Evolving With Inclusive Business in Emerging Markets

Evolving With Inclusive Business in Emerging Markets

Managing the New Bottom Line

Rajagopal

Professor, EGADE Business School

Tecnologico de Monterrey

Santa Fe Campus, Mexico City, Mexico

and

Visiting Professor

Department of Administrative Sciences

Boston University, Boston, MA

ılıBEP

BUSINESS EXPERT PRESS

Leader in applied, concise business books

With love to Arati

Description

This book discusses the attributes of inclusive business by engaging people (customers and stakeholders) in creating social and customer values and enhancing business growth among customer-centric companies.

Corporate policy and implications of the inclusiveness in businesses on social development constitute the core discussion in this book. Inclusivity concepts and arguments are endorsed by case studies across the developing economies. Philosophy and practices of inclusive business through theoretical foundations, design arguments, and managerial analysis have been discussed across five chapters.

Discussion on the success of inclusive businesses in the context of innovation, technology, and new product development which motivated people-led companies to adapt to agile business modeling and drive cocreation and coevolution initiatives is central to this book.

Keywords

inclusivity; diversity; triple bottom line; stakeholder value; cocreation; innovation management; decision making; business modeling

Contents

Testimonials

"The synergistic actions of diverse stakeholders facilitated through inclusion have proved to be the foundation of an organic growth of social and business enterprises. This book presents a conceptual framework and several case studies to validate the role of diversity and inclusion.... A good read for all in business and research."—**Hiranya K. Nath, PhD, Professor of Economics, Sam Houston State University, USA**

"Inclusivity and diversity promote the sociological perspectives of business, which is an essential platform for businesses to grow collectively. People's participation in the business is a changing scenario today.... This book exhibits the panoramic view of inclusiveness in business with real examples...." —**Jorge Pérez-Rubio Aguilar, PhD, Managing Director, México and Latin American Chapter, American Management Association**

Preface

The debate on the concept of inclusiveness in business had begun during 1990s simultaneously with the sociopolitical steering of thoughts on privatization, deregulation, and liberalization of business, which significantly affected the investment and trade regimes in the developing economies. This concept has been later adopted by the World Business Council for Sustainable Development in 2005. Inclusiveness has evolved as a business model by converging business with philanthropy and integrating the two domains to improve regional trade and economic conditions in developing countries.[1] Inclusive business practice has become central to the people's engagement in businesses and democratizes the organizational design and governance at the bottom-of-the-pyramid market segment. Nestlé in Columbia, Unilever in India, and Mary Kay Cosmetics in Mexico are growing with the inclusive business philosophy by developing design-to-society business model. Inclusive business arguably rose into prominence as a key concept toward inclusive development approach for the people at the bottom-of-the-pyramid.[2]

Thematic Discussions

The thematic discussions in this book are divided into three sections comprising the inclusive business foundation, the showcase, and business networking, across five chapters. **Chapter 1** discusses the contemporary attributes of business ecosystem and recurring shifts in the business philosophy which have transformed the business focus from power-driven (autocratic and leader-oriented) performance observed in the early

---

[1] E. Likoko and J. Kini. 2017. "Inclusive Business-a Business Approach to Development," *Current Opinion in Environmental Sustainability* 24, no. 1, pp. 84–88.

[2] J. Hall, S.V. Matos, and M.J.C. Martin. 2014. "Innovation Pathways at the Base of the Pyramid: Establishing Technological Legitimacy Through Social Attributes," *Technovation* 34, pp. 284–294.

20th century to customer centric focus, as globalization began in developing economies by the middle of the century.[3] The latter philosophy has gradually transformed businesses toward achieving a consistent growth in competitive marketplace by engaging customers. Over time, market orientation has emerged as a process with distinctive characteristics beyond the proximity to the customer. This marketing approach stresses on data gathering, the nature of the decision-making process, and implementation.[4] This chapter discusses the shifts in business ecosystem and consumer behavior because of inclusivity in business modeling. Several examples on inclusive businesses are discussed in this chapter to support arguments on inclusiveness to create social value systems for sustainable business growth. This chapter discusses various aspects of inclusivity approach in business and describes the eco-innovation as a cutting edge of the business today. The chapter concludes with the discussion on cutting edge in business observed by the customer-centric companies in emerging markets with a focus on innovation (frugal), involvement (cocreation), and integration (people-based business modeling). In addition, the case studies on Anand Milk Union Limited (AMUL) of India and Grameen Bank of Bangladesh are also discussed in this chapter.

Chapter 2 discusses the process of inclusive business design in the context of bottom-of-the-pyramid (BOP) or downstream markets. Emphasizing on inclusive business strategies, this chapter argues that cocreation is a phenomenon that helps companies in providing tailored services and higher customer satisfaction to manage business in the emerging markets.[5] This chapter discusses the process of inclusive business designing by converging the stakeholders in the BOP. This chapter argues that considering the consumer behavior and attributes of market players in the BOP market segment, there still is need for the firms to

---

[3] B. Wierenga. 2021. "The Study of Important Marketing Issues in an Evolving Field," *International Journal of Research in Marketing* 38, no. 1, pp. 18–28.

[4] B.P. Shapiro. 1988. "What the Hell Is Market Oriented?," *Harvard Business Review* 66, no. 6, pp. 119–125.

[5] For example, G. Jain, J. Paul, and A. Shrivastava. 2021. "Hyper-Personalization, Co-Creation, Digital Clienteling and Transformation," *Journal of Business Research* 124, pp. 12–23.

keep exploring the ways to effectively reach people and create value. In addition, this chapter also focuses on crowd behavior, consumer preferences, and associated values (customer and social), and explains the need for thinking out of the box to explore cocreation and coevolution prospects. Contextual to inclusive business strategies, this chapter argues that cocreation is a phenomenon that helps companies in providing tailored services and higher customer satisfaction to manage business in the emerging markets. This chapter also discusses crowd-based business modeling, shared economy, and inclusivity. The discussion on social engagement and coevolution of business are also central to this chapter. The concepts of inclusivity, cocreation, and coevolution in social enterprises have been illustrated through the case studies on energy cooperatives in Netherlands and Probiotec Agribusiness in Nepal.

The ongoing shifts in business trends indicate that most firms have already experienced the effects of deregulation, globalization, technological convergence, and the digital revolution, and have transformed the functional efficiency and market competitiveness of firms. The new milestone in managing businesses today has shifted to collective intelligence and crowd behavior, which helps firms in cocreation and coevolution process.[6] **Chapter 3** discusses various people's perspectives that contribute to collective intelligence and decision making in the customer-centric firms. Community workspaces in rural and semiurban demographics in developing countries encourage inclusive business initiatives and crowd-based business modeling. The crowd behavior contributes to a new range of business opportunities by building democratic business philosophy as *for the people and by the people*. Consequently, the crowdsourcing practices in businesses have led to the emergence of populist business models, which leads to deliver competitive advantage, while simultaneously presenting new challenges to entrepreneurs and executives.[7] Continuing the discussion contextual to the crowd-based business

---

[6] C.K. Prahalad and V. Ramaswamy. 2000. "Co-Opting Customer Competence," *Harvard Business Review* 78, no. 1, pp. 79–87.

[7] K. Täuscher. 2017. "Leveraging Collective Intelligence: How to Design and Manage Crowd-Based Business Models," *Business Horizons* 60, no. 2, pp. 237–245.

modeling, this chapter emphasizes the role of inclusive marketing-mix comprising people, psychodynamics, pace (first mover advantage), performance, and posture (corporate reputation) as an integrated tool for business decisions. Discussions on reverse accountability in monitoring performance in people-led business firms, which supplements the leadership perspectives on inclusive business, are also addressed in this chapter. Such governance system creates competitive advantage through higher customer value and contributes to business growth of the company and society.[8] This chapter discusses the attributes of community workplace, experience sharing, and collective intelligence. In addition, the discussion on inclusive marketing-mix and corporate social responsibility also leads the chapter. There are three case studies discussed in this chapter comprising ITC Agribusiness (India), Shakti experiment of Hindustan Unilever Limited (India), and Sodexo, a French food services and facilities companies.

In the section on the inclusive business showcase, **Chapter 4** converses on continuous learning as the vital process in social and customer-centric businesses. This chapter emphasizes how lessons can be drawn from the success and failure experiences in doing business with people. The pace at which organizations learn may become the only sustainable source of competitive advantage over time.[9] The participatory business appraisal as a new concept has been discussed as a continuous learning tool by engaging customers, stake holders, and crowd within the business ecosystem. Participatory appraisals are used as a driver to actions research in resolving social issues and analyzing the cultural, biological, and legal perspectives to promote customer centric businesses on a social scale.[10] Continuing the discussion on community participation, the chapter discusses the role of voice of customers, lifetime value, and perceptual semantics as the

---

[8] N.M.P. Bocken, S.W. Short, P. Rana, and S. Evans. 2014. "A Literature and Practice Review to Develop Sustainable Business Model Archetypes," *Journal of Cleaner Production* 65, no. 1, pp. 42–56.

[9] P.M. Senge. 1990. "Leader's New Work: Building Learning Organizations," *MIT Sloan Management Review* 32, no. 1, pp. 7–23.

[10] For example, R. Chambers. 1994. "The Origins and Practice of Participatory Rural Appraisal," *World Development* 22, no. 7, pp. 953–969.

drivers of customer behavior. This chapter discusses the broad perspectives of continuous learning and its effects on organizational culture. The role of organizational learning on design thinking and systems thinking is also discussed in this chapter. The process of developing organizational mission and vision has also been discussed in the context of organizational learning and thinking philosophies. The two case studies on Mukamas, a Finnish learning agglomerate, and GE bottom-up communications endorse the concepts of continuous learning, design thinking, and systems thinking that are discussed in this chapter.

Chapter 5 discusses social business modeling and the role of transformational leadership in the context of profitability and growth. Social enterprises aim to create both social and financial value, through the people-led business models that allow sustainable growth. These enterprises innovate their business models through multiple activities over time and tailor them to produce social and financial values.[11] The social consciousness in business has also been discussed in this chapter as an ecosystem of inclusive business, which helps firms tackling poverty and inequality at the bottom-of-the-pyramid segment. The chapter argues that inclusive business generates revenues through social marketing to create social value among stakeholders and surrounding communities.[12] This chapter discusses social business modeling and the role of transformational leadership in the context of profitability and growth. In addition, this chapter exhibits synergy pyramid comprising interconnectivity among planning, customer, and strategic alliances. The chapter argues that inclusive business generates revenues through social marketing to create social value among stakeholders and surrounding communities. In addition, this chapter discusses the factors affecting the changing consumer behavior and entrepreneurial growth in social business.

---

[11] S. Tykkyläinen and P. Ritala. 2021. "Business Model Innovation in Social Enterprises: An Activity System Perspective," *Journal of Business Research* 125, pp. 684–697.

[12] F.M. Santos. 2012. "A Positive Theory of Social Entrepreneurship," *Journal of Business Ethics* 111, pp. 335–351.

Discussion Paradigm

This book discusses the attributes of inclusive business by engaging people (customers and stakeholders) in creating social and customer values and enhancing business growth for *profit with performance* among customer-centric companies. The effects of the inclusiveness in businesses on social development and growth through triple and quadruple bottom-lines constitute the core discussion in this book. Coevolution and value creation have been explained as the crowd-based business approach, which benefits companies in the long term. This book argues various dimensions of inclusive business and suggests ways in developing collective business models with alternate thinking to build market competitiveness. The discussion model of the book is exhibited in Figure P-1.

This book discusses the philosophy and practices of inclusive business through theoretical foundations, design arguments, and managerial analysis as illustrated in Figure P-1. The concept of inclusive business has been explained in the context of the various ecosystems that affect the business orientation and functionality of firms. Consequently, business, social, crowd, and behavioral ecosystems significantly contribute to the attributes of business inclusiveness. These ecosystems are built on triple and quadruple bottom-lines as explained in the following figure. Most companies that are currently engaged in building inclusiveness in business aim at earning profit with people, purpose, and sustainability (triple bottom-line), while some companies tend to complement the inclusive business approaches with people, reverse accountability, organizational control (social), and transformational initiatives (quadruple bottom-line). This book discusses the success of inclusive businesses in the context of innovation, technology, and new product development which motivated people-led companies to adapt to agile business modelling and drive cocreation and coevolution initiatives. The inclusive business approach has been critically examined in this book with a focus on people's perspectives as illustrated in Figure P-1. Developing "out-of-the-box" strategies for inclusive businesses has also been discussed in the book explaining the crowd behavior, market competition, consumer needs, preferences, and associated values.

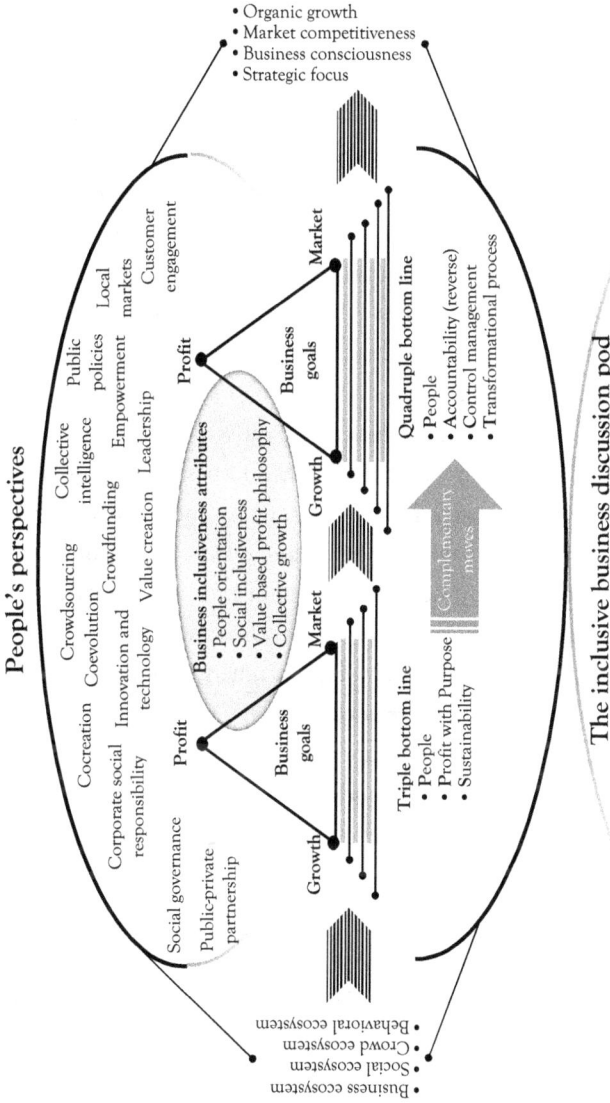

Figure P-1 Discussion paradigm of the book

Source: Author

Value Perspectives

This book discusses the socialization of business as a corporate philosophy to understand people in general and customers and stakeholders in particular to motivate cocreating value-based business performance. Reviewing a wide range of literature from empirical research studies to best practices followed by the companies, this book analyzes the emerging theories of inclusiveness in business, corporate social responsibility, social learning, and value cocreation. The concepts and models developed in the book are central to people's involvement, and their engagement in business with the increase in social-responsive behavior of companies to support coevolution of business with customers and stakeholders. Thematically, the discussion on these perspectives is interpreted as an inclusive business process with multilayered marketing strategies across various geodemographic segments. The focus of the discussion on inclusive business is precisely on using collective intelligence and collective performance through social networks, leadership, and crowd consciousness. This book deliberates upon critical success factors of firms, which include diversity and cross-functionality by managing the triple and quadruple bottom-line. It is argued in the book that timely deployment of streamlined crowd-based marketing strategies in chaotic markets could enhance the effects of social innovation, increase value spread among consumers, and reduce growing complexities in the global and regional markets. Collective intelligence creates intrinsic and extrinsic motivation with distinctive effects on prosocial behavior, which helps firms to understand the effects of crowd behavior.[13] This book presents new insights on developing inclusive business models using both aggressive (crowd-driven) and defensive (competitive) marketing strategies in the inclusive business models. The book guides managers on both marketing tactics and strategies using the 5Ts concepts for managing time (first mover advantage), territory (new market segments), target (potential consumers), thrust (competitive), and tasks (cocreation).

---

[13] A. Festré and P. Garrouste. 2015. "Theory and Evidence in Psychology and Economics About Motivation Crowding Out: A Possible Convergence?," *Journal of Economic Survey* 29, no. 2, pp. 339–356.

This book presents case studies on inclusive businesses across the developing countries including Asia, Europe, Africa, and Latin America. Case studies are discussed in relevant chapters to support the discussions on various aspects of inclusive business. Each chapter is provided with an overview of the discussions and the summary at the end. The visual map of concepts and strategies on inclusive business is supported by the creative figures and appropriate data in each chapter. Such illustrations make this book appealing for readers and offers smooth transition in learning. This book bridges theory and applications of inclusive businesses practices by linking crowd behavior, market competition, and customer value in managing multilayered marketing paradigms to achieve strategic business performance and market competitiveness. Inclusive business modeling with these elements tends to reduce chaotic effects, decision imperfections, and negativity on consumer values. This book argues the need for companies to understand about achieving an inner analytic edge to defend value-driven business and augment market share. Though companies draw some competition-based decisions through performance dashboards, the book reviews logical framework analysis and consumer-centered strategies for making sustainable decisions. Customer engagement has emerged as a core concept in developing marketing strategies though significant research on inclusive business in the context of emotion-decision equilibrium has been limited.[14] This book specifically discusses the following attributes of the inclusive businesses in building effective business models:

- Linking business with societal modes to reduce whiplashes with the conventional innovation-marketing matrix
- Developing inclusive business into consumer centric perspectives to strengthen social foundation
- Growing firms as first movers and reaping competitive advantage by developing collective business strategies and build "value-defensive" models

---

[14] M. Kleinaltenkamp, I.O. Karpen, C. Plewa, E. Jaakkola, and J. Conduit. 2019. "Collective Engagement in Organizational Settings," *Industrial Marketing Management* 80, no. 1, pp. 11–23.

- Understanding cognitive ergonomics of consumers to develop value-led business performance
- Developing collective engagement in business settings

Though inclusive business is a collective concept, it is often viewed as a social growth of firms. The inclusive value proposition is described as a synergy between society and business in this book, which asserts that people-led business models reap strategic benefits. Building and maintaining synergy in inclusive businesses is an ongoing process through cooperative and collaborative activities, and programs to create and enhance mutual economic value. This perspective is emphasized in the context of for-profit and not-for-profit organizations. The book argues that companies need to consider a broader social perspective to enhance the effectiveness of business models by implementing applied marketing decisions and putting the consumer first in the business management process. This book connects the social perspectives of companies in emerging markets with business performance matrix across geodemographic segments.

Principal audience of this book are managers, researchers, and students of marketing strategy, marketing research, business analytics, and courses in decision sciences. This book has been developed also to serve as a managerial guide and think tank for the graduate students engaged in studying courses on business strategy and marketing. Besides serving as a reference book to the students, this would also be an inspiring book for managers, market analysts, and business consultants engaged in decision-making process for developing marketing strategy. This book will contribute to the existing literature and deliver new concepts to the students and researchers to pursue the subject further. By reading this book, working managers may also realize how to converge best practices with corporate strategies in managing business at the destination markets while students would learn the new dimensions of marketing strategies.

Rajagopal
Mexico City
April 01, 2022

Acknowledgments

In completing this volume of the book, I have been benefitted by the discussions of my colleagues within and outside the EGADE Business School. I am thankful to Dr. Osmar Hazael Zavaleta Vazquez, Associate Dean of Research at EGADE Business School, Mexico, who has been encouraging to my new endeavors. I thank all my students of graduate and doctoral programs at EGADE Business School for sharing enriching ideas on the subject during the classroom discussions, which helped in building this book on the framework of innovative ideas. This book is an outgrowth of my teaching new concepts in qualitative research to doctoral research scholars and working managers in the MBA program.

I also acknowledge the outstanding support of Scott Isenberg, Executive Editor of Business Expert Press, who critically examined the proposal, guided the manuscript preparation, and took the publication process forward. I am thankful to various anonymous referees of my previous research works on innovation and technology management that helped me in looking deeper into the conceptual gaps and improving the quality with their valuable comments. Though it was a solo journey with this publication project from ideation to manuscript preparation, I must acknowledge the encouragement from senior academics to proceed ahead with the project. I express my deep gratitude to my wife Arati Rajagopal, who always reminded me of this task over other deadlines in the agenda. She also deserves kudos for copy editing the manuscript rigorously before submitting it to the publisher.

CHAPTER 1

The Concept Map

Contemporary attributes of business ecosystem and recurring shifts in the business philosophy, which have transformed the business focus from power-driven (autocratic and leader-oriented) performance observed in the early-twentieth century to customer-centric focus as globalization, began in developing economies by the middle of the century. The latter philosophy has gradually transformed businesses toward achieving a consistent growth in competitive marketplace by engaging stakeholders. Over time, market orientation has been emerged as a process with distinctive characteristics beyond the proximity to the customer through inclusivity in business. Such business approach has been based on collective intelligence, stakeholder involvement and participatory decision-making process, and implementation. This chapter discusses the shifts in business ecosystem and consumer behavior because of inclusivity in business modeling. Several examples on inclusive businesses are discussed in this chapter to support arguments on inclusiveness to create social value systems for sustainable business growth. This chapter discusses various aspects of inclusivity approach in business and describes the eco-innovation as a cutting edge of the business today. The discussions reveals that the inclusive business options have emerged as sustainable solutions in community business activities at the bottom-of-the-pyramid (BOP) such as cooperative organizations as the core social business model. In addition, this chapter also discusses the contextual effects of triple bottom line comprising people, profit with purpose, and sustainability, and PACT elements (people, accountability, control, and transformation) of quadruple bottom line. The chapter concludes with the discussion on cutting edge in business observed by the customer-centric companies in emerging markets with focus on innovation (frugal), involvement (cocreation), and integration (people-based business modeling). In addition, the case studies on Anand Milk Union Limited (AMUL) of India and Grameen Bank of Bangladesh are also discussed in this chapter.

Business Ecosystem

The business paradigms at global, regional, and niche levels have been continuously shifting within business ecosystems on temporal and spatial dimensions. In this process, the stakeholders are the key influencers on the shifts and innovation of a firm's business model. Drawing insights from the changing business ecosystem in the context of growing technology, business governance, and resource-based business strategies, the stakeholders have been affecting the firm's business model innovation (BMI) and relationships with customers, stakeholders, and the key partners. Working under the changing business ecosystems, the firms have often become learning organizations and adapted to the systems thinking. The business models have moved today far from conventional competency-based approach to resource view-based, crowed-based, and agile business modeling practices. Consequently, at every transition, BMI has emerged as a major challenge for the firms in integrating temporal and spatial goals. The BMI challenges involve holistic changes in the structure and complex tasks in creating new businesses, delivering products and services, and capturing value. The frequent shift in business models has attracted considerable scholarly attention and managerial efforts toward increasing a firm's competitive advantages (Yi et al. 2022). Continuous transition of business models of the firms over time in emerging markets has significantly moved the locus of value creation and value capture to the changing business ecosystems. Accordingly, the stakeholders (e.g., customers, competitors, suppliers, social organizations, and other institutions) and the key partners play an important role in determining (cocreating), implementing (coevolution), and monitoring (reverse accountability) the performance of businesses. Firms strengthen the relationships among all stakeholders associated with the business organizations as they increasingly rely on stakeholders within the business ecosystem to cocreate and capture value by redesigning inclusive and crowd-based business models (Wei et al. 2017).

The business ecosystem standpoint has evolved with the increasing technologies, administering experimental business models such as agile, inclusive, and crowd-based business models. Such transitions in business modeling suggest that firms focus on acquiring survival skills within expanding networks of stakeholders and grow on the triple bottom line comprising people (stakeholders), planet (sustainability), and profit (driving profit with purpose). The business model of any type is primarily aimed at achieving competitive advantages in a networked context, and firms tend to leverage value creation through a wider network of the key partners as well (Park et al. 2017). Therefore, BMI is a continuous process involving stakeholders and key partners to gain competitive advantages. The stakeholder relationship and value propositions are important for firms to differentiate the performance and business expansion strategies. Intrafirm and industry stakeholders often offer knowledge and information through collective intelligence platforms, while the gatekeepers (outside of firm or industry) provide competitive knowledge and novel (or radical) ideas for business growth (e.g., Yi et al. 2022). To manage business to gain profit within the ecosystems, companies need to clearly identify the performance milestones, key activities, and key partners. In addition, firms need to establish efficient stage-gates (for setting goals and review objectives) to improve the business models (Williamson and De Meyer 2022). The core and auxiliary elements of business ecosystem are illustrated in Figure 1.1.

The core elements of business ecosystem include stakeholders, competition, social factors, and business taxonomy as exhibited in Figure 1.1. The stakeholders are engaged in cocreation and coevolution of innovation within the business firms. In customer-centric firms, stakeholders also participate in the organizational governance. Firms face aggressive competition for the products and services in the high-demand portfolios, while the low-cost defender companies secure their operations in the niche. The hybridity in market competition has emerged as cooperative cooperation (*coopetition*), which encourages firms to develop collaborative strategies with the competing firms to gain a win-win bargain. The auxiliary element of business ecosystem consists of BMI, business transition, business philosophy, and innovation and technology (Martin et al. 2021). The innovation in business model is a continuous process, and it is emerging in customer-centric and collaborative strategy development with selected competing firms (cooptation strategy). In

Innovation and technology
• Cocreation
• Frugal innovation
• Reverse innovation
• PNS factors
• Technology cost and life cycle

Stakeholders
• Engagement
• Cocreation
• Coevolution with organization
• Governance

Business model innovation
• Customer centric strategies
• Cooperative competition
• Agile business practice
• Dynamic operations
• Market integration

Competition
• Aggressive
• Defensive
• Low-cost defenders
• Hybrid
• Cooptation

Business transitions
• Business dynamics
• Mergers and acquisitions
• Darwinian fitness
• Market taxonomy
  • Upstream
  • Big-middle
  • Bottom-of-the-pyramid
• Leadership

Social factors
• Values and lifestyle
• Entrepreneurship
• Inclusivity
• Social governance
• Social responsibility

Business taxonomy
• Business-to-consumer
• Business-to-business
• Consumer-to-consumer
• Online-to-offline
• Omni channel strategy
• Social media marketing

Business philosophy
• Triple bottom line
• People, planet and profit
• PACT
  • People, accountability, control, and transformation
• Inclusivity in business

Business Ecosystem

Core

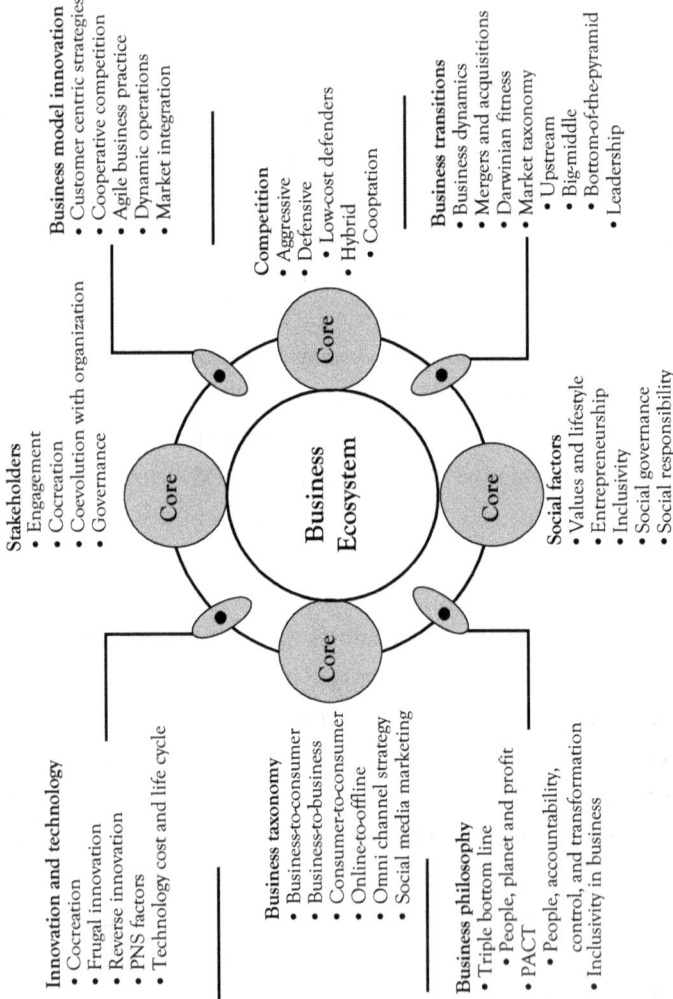

Figure 1.1 Elements of business ecosystem

Source: Author

addition, most customer-centric companies such as LEGO, Cisco, and Barclays have switched to agile business practices, while some companies like Apple and Coca-Cola have practiced the integrated marketing strategies. In the process of business innovation, firms have also faced transition across the market segments across upstream, *big-middle*, and BOP. The business philosophy of the firms has also changed over time from competitive business focus to inclusivity in business. In addition, the triple bottom line emphasizing the integration of people, planet, and profit has reinforced the concept of inclusivity, stakeholder accountability, and transformation.

The business ecosystem today has observed a radical shift due to manifold growth of information and communication technology and extensive digitization of business processes. Such radical shift in businesses has been induced by the increased use of Internet to stimulate the ambidextrous digitization at the corporate and stakeholder levels. The dependency on web-based technologies has brought disruptive changes to the spatial landscape of business through the creation of an entire host of digital marketing tactics, customer convenience, and competitiveness. Managers of the firm need to prioritize the development of preferred business models they wish to work with and determine which technology to adopt in marketing practices to gain both strategic and tactical leverage. The business competition has a complex grid of prospectors, analyzers, low-cost defenders, and differentiated defenders. Prospector firms gain the first mover advantage of new products or services and initially play tactics to leapfrog competitors' offerings develop. These firms attempt to lead the market and stay differentiated among the challengers and follower firms in the marketplace. They typically push their business to premium niche and operate with limited production and distribution. The prospector firms include Tesla, Cisco, and others. Similarly, Apple emerged initially as a prospector firm and over time expanded its market to the *big-middle* consumer segment with a consistent lead in the market against its rivals in the consumer electronics product portfolio. The prospector firms extensively use social media marketing, data-driven personalization, e-mail marketing, and marketing technology. Successful competing firms broadly scan markets to identify the consumer needs, demand, and required differentiators to establish the strategic and tactical lead in the market.

The defender firms largely play on price and promotion perspectives to sustain the fierce market competition. These firms operate on low-cost control and play defensive to secure their market share by delivering high value among the customers. Low-cost defender firms often offer customer-centric services to operate consistently in the markets. The analyzer firms such as Walmart focus on offering products or services of the acceptable quality and tend to inculcate trust among customers by building strong and consistent corporate posture (in case of Walmart, the posture is "Everyday low prices"). Similarly, the analyzer firms at the upstream markets such as Marks and Spenser (UK), Macy's (USA), and Liverpool (Mexico) typically charge substantial premium and focus on a niche within the *big-middle* segments and customers that are relatively affluent. These firms often operate in high- or middle-end customer segments and focus on developing long-term relationships with customers. Other firms in this category include Proctor & Gamble, Unilever, and Tiffany & Co (Olson et al. 2021).

Digital technology has enabled shoppers to expand their outreach to customers and develop hybrid marketing strategies by supporting online-to-offline (O-to-O) business model. Accordingly, the firms develop convergence with the online marketing strategies, sellers, and customers by understanding their preferences and needs. Customer-centric companies extensively use social media channels and new mobile tools to educate consumers on digital marketing trends and benefits. In addition, firms reengineer their processes and organizational structures to proactively lead digital markets and stimulate customers toward making buying decisions and beyond. Building successful digitization journeys requires firms to develop capabilities on smooth transition of conventional practices to digitization environment, automation of brick-and-mortar processes to online or hybrid formats, customization of services to create value among the stakeholders, continuous interactions with stakeholders and potential customers to develop emotional engagement, inculcating the stakeholder and customer loyalty to construct the business defense line against competitions. In addition, the most successful companies tend to integrate designers, developers, data analysts, marketers, and others to create and implement agile business models, which help in achieving overall business performance of the firm (Edelman and Singer 2015).

The industry attractiveness was conventionally analyzed in the context of threats from new entrants, substitution effects for products and services, and bargaining power of buyers and suppliers. However, such analysis has become precise and simple with the hybrid business models, which describes online-to-offline (O-to-O) competition, profit optimization, and value-chain management. The O-to-O competition is also explained as platform businesses that bring together consumers and producers as Uber, Alibaba, and Airbnb do, which requires a different approach to strategy. The platform business is a good example for growing inclusivity in business. The critical asset of a platform is the wide range of stakeholders associated with the crowd. The network effects are orchestrated by the crowd-based stakeholders, who collaborate with the firms in developing marketing strategies, implementation by market, and inculcating value chain among the stakeholders (Van Alstyne et al. 2016). Systemic thinking framework impacts the business environment in which firms operate in a fluid, dynamic, and interdependent way. This approach contrasts with the linear approach commonly used in business and other disciplines and offers practical solutions and guidance for business leaders to incorporate complexity science into creating sustainable businesses (Sun et al. 2018).

In the growing competitive market of mobile communications today, Xiaomi pushed into the market by generating significant customer value in the home market, which helped the company to leapfrog to become one of China's leading smartphone manufacturing and marketing company after its kick-off to consumer electronics market in 2010. The company rose into prominence by establishing its business posture as price and technology leader. Consequently, the company was looking to strengthen its market share by recovering the declining repeat purchase rate and reviving its brand impact of its products. Later Xiaomi planned to invest heavily in an ecosystem of key partners by identifying allied companies and compatible smart products. Xiaomi has also evaluated the pros and cons of its Internet-based sales model and determined business-to-business and online-to-offline business models. Such alternatives helped the company drive growth and plan investment in the full-fledged retail network across the countries (Dann et al. 2017).

The functional ecosystems can be categorized as extended enterprises and platform markets (emerging out of platform economy), which lead to the distinct governance of local, regional, and global business hubs. The extended enterprises integrate the key partners in the business ecosystem of the firm to develop and manage value chain. In a platform market, the "platform hub" defines and supplies architecture to facilitate the innovation of both core and complementary products with an objective to expand the outreach and value of customers in using the business platform (Rong et al. 2021). The platform economy and market are emerged out of the e-commerce concept and have expanded to O-to-O business model by integrating the brick-and-mortar business with the online transactions. Accordingly, the customers on both extended enterprise and platform market business models will be motivated to get associated with value-based products or services to develop consumption culture congruent with the product offerings of the company. In other words, the platform market represents an ambidextrous business model in which the crowd and potential customers could have interactive dialogues (Visnjic et al. 2016).

Many companies in emerging markets have managed to develop competitive differentiation to stay ahead of multinational companies. Local companies customize products and services to meet ethnic consumer needs and slowly follow the economies of scale. Small emerging companies develop business models to overcome market-specific difficulties and attempt to gain competitive advantage against the multinational brands in the marketplace over the time. However, consumer prefers to stay with the companies, who deliver products and services with the latest technologies and augment competitive advantage. Regional companies gain price leadership quickly as they find ways to support low-price strategy through the low-cost labor and offering in-house training to their employees in lieu of hiring skilled employees, which escalate costs. However, they invest in top management talent to drive rapid growth. Successful home-grown champions that have grown global include a few multinationals, such as Yum Brands, Nokia, and Hyundai, have managed to overturn the local competitors by using the above organizational and marketing management strategies (Bhattacharya and Michael 2008).

Shifts in Consumer Behavior

Interactive learning is a psycho-social phenomenon influenced by the technological and social trends. Learning and adaptation to many real-world applications, like computer and mobile applications on services and entertainments, depend on cognitive affective states (emotions). Affective states are complex psycho-physiological and psycho-social constructs comprising valence, arousal, and motivational intensity (Salgado and Clempner 2018). People develop association with the technological innovations on social motivation and self-reference based on individual rationale. However, rationality alone is not adequate for successful adaptation of technological innovations. Emotions also influence the processes of rational decision making and manifesting human intelligence. Learning is a continuous process as described in the marketing literature. It is the process by which behavioral changes occur as a cognitive appraisal of experience on usefulness of technology. In the interactive learning process, emotions affect the customer value and influence the intention to adapt to technological innovations (Kim et al. 2016).

Switching from shopping in physical stores to virtual retail outlets is a slow transition among elderly consumers as compared to the young consumers. In practice, consumers are gaining a wide range of benefits such as quick comparisons on price and quality of products, online promotions, peer motivation on adapting to retailing technology, increased shopping enjoyment, and improved perceived value by embracing the virtual retailing technology. In a physical store, consumer derives motivation through sensory stimuli that affect the five senses (i.e., vision, hearing, touch, smell, and taste) and induce the desire to shop. On the other hand, environmental stimuli are restricted to affecting vision or hearing in an online store (Lo et al. 2016). Peer interactions not only provide customers the confidence in decision making but also let them express their perceptions and experience of product and services through a social channel. Consequently, peer motivation encourages customers to adapt to innovative retailing technologies like augmented reality, quick response (QR) codes to obtain comprehensive product information, self-controlled checkouts, and managing product deliveries. The e-word-of-mouth communication is central to peer motivations, which influences customers' attitudes and behaviors before and during shopping. Complexity of information on the website sometimes attributes to the uncertainties about the product quality or service, which drives the customer to consider experiences of other consumers (Mudambi and Schuff 2010). The digital communications through social media channels and blogs of customer communities have emerged today as the guiding tools for customers to make online shopping decisions such as choosing the shopping outlets that are less complicated, contain wide product portfolios, and are trustworthy. The peer information leads customers to stay attentive to crowd-cognitive insights and consumption patterns to evaluate the self-reference and develop conformity with the online shopping decisions (Lamberton and Stephen 2016).

Customers learn to shop online by using retailing technologies and by interacting with companies and peers on e-commerce platforms individually and with friends and family. The interactive retailing technologies enhance customer-learning in group with online communities that support social connection to enhance conversation between customers. Information search for online shopping provides the customers a wide scope of learning about the product attributes and company profile, and helps the associated market players such as service providers comprehend the rationale of buying and decision making (Chen et al. 2017). Customers learn comprehensively about products and services online by extensive navigation, which is like window shopping. The interactive websites and live conversations with the retailers help in transferring the knowledge on products and services from the vendor's website to a consumer. Interactive visual aids like 3-D presentations managed in a timely manner help customers acquire visual information on products online. Interactive learning is delayed in visualizing multiple product images as they require multiple clicks to reach the desirable information and due to product differences (Khakimdjanova and Park 2005).

As the competition in online shopping has increased manifold with localized digital applications and retailing logistics, physical stores are complementing their existing business models with online shopping and low-cost personalized deliveries within a predetermined geographic radius to enhance the customer experience. Interactive displays, touch screens, easy check-out functionality, and virtual informative touchpoints have been enhanced and adopted to augment customer engagement and experiences with online retailing process. The interactive displays, 3-D virtual experience, and augmented reality websites of companies provide real-time interactivity to customers (Kim et al. 2016). Despite attractive retailing technologies, the core encircling issues that call for attention of retailers are about how useful these technologies are to customers, how the customers perceive its usefulness and ease of use, and derive the best value out of the online buying behavior. The impact of smart retail technologies on the customer experience drives the performance of businesses during the pandemic-led business-shutdown situation. Retail technologies are adopted by the companies in view of their cost, contribution to the sales, and ease of use to the customers. Retailers place emphasis on customer-centric technologies designed to cut costs and make shopping a memorable experience to their customers (Pantano and Viassone 2014). The major attributes causing the shifts in consumer behavior and their effects on business performance have been exhibited in Figure 1.2.

Shifts in the consumer behavior are largely affected by the global trends in social health (diet and general well-being), conscious consumption (green products and services), sustainability (planet and ecology), and technology (green and utilitarian values) as exhibited in Figure 1.2. The global trends have driven the PNS factors through emotions, vogue, social dynamics, and peer pressure over time. Consequently, cognition and personality among consumers are influenced by the collective intelligence and crowd behavior. Consumers learn by analyzing the product, market, and crowd information, and establish the competitive differentiators contextual to the self-actualization and satisfaction. In addition, social and technological factors such as digitization, e-commerce, hybrid business platforms, social media, and crowd behavior have significantly shifted the consumer behavior. Knowledge sharing, empowerment (inclusivity), and self and social perceptions drive consumer behavior in the context of changing marketing attributes (Laursen and Salter 2006).

Mobile technology applications have stimulated consumers in evaluating the competing offerings, using interactive technology to reaffirm buying decisions and making purchases, and engaging with on-site client services to resolve any product or delivery conflicts. Transformation

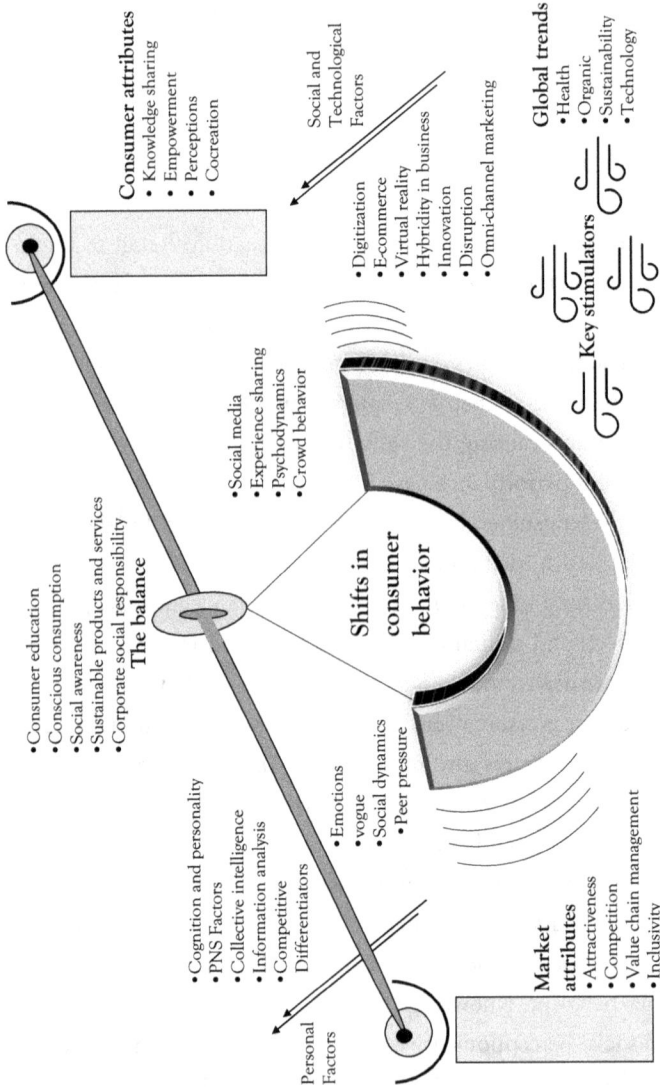

Consumer attributes
- Knowledge sharing
- Empowerment
- Perceptions
- Cocreation

Social and
Technological
Factors

- Digitization
- E-commerce
- Virtual reality
- Hybridity in business
- Innovation
- Disruption
- Omni-channel marketing

Global trends
- Health
- Organic
- Sustainability
- Technology

Key stimulators

- Social media
- Experience sharing
- Psychodynamics
- Crowd behavior

Shifts in consumer behavior

- Consumer education
- Conscious consumption
- Social awareness
- Sustainable products and services
- Corporate social responsibility

The balance

- Cognition and personality
- PNS Factors
- Collective intelligence
- Information analysis
- Competitive Differentiators

- Emotions
- vogue
- Social dynamics
- Peer pressure

Personal
Factors

Market attributes
- Attractiveness
- Competition
- Value chain management
- Inclusivity

Figure 1.2 Shifts in consumer behavior: causes and effects

Source: Author

of retailing services such as 360° product views and features, informational touch points, interactive displays, and applications for mobile devices has increased the perceived usefulness of these technology attributes among consumers (Grewal et al. 2017). In the business lockdown, retailers focused on e-commerce as the active transactional channel over the existing physical stores. However, the omnichannel approach to retailing remained effective in creating unified experience between the brick-and-mortar and online channels including interactive web stores (Steinhoff et al. 2019). Retail technologies are increasingly encouraging customers to gain new experience in comprehending product attributes, their fit to the needs, value for money, and shopping enjoyment using the technology-based self-service. In addition, customers have access to the extended information on products and stores by scanning the QR codes associated with the physical products that are delivered to customers. The scanning of QR codes provides customers a one-touch comprehensive information on the products purchased and increases the usefulness of technology, while retailers benefit from reducing the cost and time to share on real-time product and market information with the customer through conventional channels. Customers find the use of QR codes with smartphone applications easy and can analyze information categorically. Retailing technologies that focus on QR, just-in-time, ease of use, and direct delivery attract customers to shop with confidence. In addition, customer services provide higher usefulness of retailing technologies and customer satisfaction. However, from the point of view of retailers, cost efficiency is the priority focus for implementing innovative technology (Shin et al. 2012).

Retailing technology today has also encouraged customers to redeem their promotional coupons online, which has not only helped in developing customer loyalty to retail organizations or brands but also helped retailers increase their volume of sales. The usage of promotional coupons elicits emotions, peer influence, purchase intentions, and repeat buying behavior among customers (Khachatryan et al. 2018). The price-discount factors influence impulsive buying behavior among consumers, and impulsiveness tends to develop positive cognitive enactments. However, impulsive purchases often create initial distrust and dissonance among customers during an online coupon-purchase due to intangibility of the reward and redemption of promotion coupons online. Electronic coupons induce both positive and negative effects depending on the reputation of online retailing company and the fairness of discounts or promotion offered to a specific product. In online retailing, e-coupons are mainly circulated as scratch-code-based coupons, e-mail coupons, and promotional coupons (Li et al. 2019). E-promotions through couponing drive impulsive purchases without any prior planning. Impulsive purchase is primarily driven by the assortment of products in the online store and promotions. Price and volume promotions through redemption of coupons involve both planned and impulsive buying behavior. Some studies have revealed that impulsiveness is largely driven through reward-seeking behavior (Balakrishnan et al. 2020).

Design elements influence decision-making process of buying online products and reducing the self-control of consumers or enhance the possibility of impulsive buying. Online store design helps in developing relationship between design elements and consumer purchase intention (Lo et al. 2016). Ease-of-use website interfaces reduce the cognitive load of consumers during shopping navigation and acquiring required information. Most websites consisting of product pictures, videos, and interactive tools to augment product usage complement the text descriptions and increase the scope of product recognition among customers. Appropriate organization of products in arrays and well-organized display (Verhagen and van Dolen 2011) in online stores may make the shopping navigation interesting and reduce the stress in product search among customers. Customers sometimes find it difficult to view high-resolution product images on retailing website due to limitations of Internet bandwidth. However, clarity of product images helps consumers formulate their product expectations in lieu of the routine practice of touch, feel, and pick in the physical stores. Retail websites with colorful layouts, categorical arrays of products, back and forth navigation with retention of previous searches, interactive tools, and online chat rooms are perceived by customers as quality online platforms. Price comparisons across products with similar attributes in the online store not only support buying decisions among customers but also build trust and perceived transparency on the retailing company. The quality of retailing websites, therefore, integrates usefulness of retailing technologies, impulsive buying, and deriving value for money among customers (Lo et al. 2016).

Continuous innovation and technology in the consumer products companies have set new trends in the market and created dynamic value perceptions among consumers that have raised their preferences and expectations. Digital marketing has opened massive opportunities to deliver new consumer experiences and strengthened the relationships with consumers across the destinations in the global marketplace. Digital disruption has created new dimensions in consumer marketing through the benefits of large-scale promotions and convenience to drive compulsive buying behavior among consumers. The platform economy has shown a huge shift in the creation of consumer value. However, technology and born-digital businesses have led the innovations, which is being experienced by consumers in every sector now. The platform economy distinctly comprises a new set of business and economic relations that depend on the Internet, computation, and data (Hein et al. 2020). The ecosystem created by each platform is a source of value, and it sets the terms, by which users can participate. Such business and economic platform has empowered consumers and developed their bargaining potential for quality and value for money. Though digitalization in marketing has induced rapid shift in the consumer behavior through open access to brand communication, consumer experiences, and socio-psychological cognition toward building their preferences and values, many multinationals are encouraging "value-chain localization" strategies which still focus on only the premier segment of consumers. This strategy does not adequately prepare them to meet the greater challenge and opportunity of reaching out the remote consumers and achieving the universe of market by serving the consumers of all segments including premier, mass (upper, regular, and lower stratum), and BOP. Hindustan Unilever Limited (HUL), a consumer products company, has extensively reached the consumers at the BOP, to market its consumer brands by empowering rural women as sales representatives. HUL has created consumer behavior for its brands upholding gender and societal values.

Most companies are inculcating radical buying behavior among consumers by generating brand literacy through the interactions of consumer communities on social media. Facebook, Twitter, and Instagram have been the principal platforms of consumer networking for most of the consumer-centric companies. Companies explore the consumer needs and preferences on the digital platforms and tend to meet consumers' rising expectations on the products and services they intend to buy. Simultaneously, to reaffirm their purchase intentions, consumers also stay critical to the multichannel experience of peers on their preferred brands. The consumer experience is diffused by the user-generated contents on social media, which help them review their perceptions, attitude, and behavior toward a brand in the marketplace. Social platforms support consumer knowledge and learning process on product innovation and create positive influence on community learning process. Such knowledge transfer practice implies that firms can stimulate communication and interaction among people (Carmona-Lavado et al. 2013). Social media and peer reviews deliver knowledge directly on products and services, which helps in consumer learning process and enhances their decision-making skills. The participatory learning model as demonstrated by the community, family, and social media platforms not only helps consumers in acquiring information and knowledge on brands and markets but also constitutes consumer behavior. Consumer knowledge leads them to explore new products and user opportunities, influence cognitive abilities, and draw motivations for experimenting new consumerism models. The causes or gaps in the transfer of brand knowledge between consumers and media often distract the consumer learning process. Consumers learn about product, services, and new consumption patterns through community resources. The community learning process prompts coshopping and coviewing of brands in the marketplace, which stimulates consumers to also review the referrals and conform to community decisions. Hence, most referral programs of the consumer products companies focus on diffusing brand awareness among the family or community as a source of knowledge hub of consumers (Neeley 2005). Therefore, most companies tend to transfer brand through knowledge management practices following efficient handling of information and resources within the organization and empowering consumer communities in diffusing the knowledge. By enhancing the consumer engagement and adopting systematic dissemination of knowledge, consumer groups like lead users and early majority acquire adequate awareness about the new products and services and stimulate buying decisions by experimenting them. Such efforts of a company tend to minimize or eliminate knowledge transfer gaps and improve market competitiveness and performance of the brands and the company (Rajagopal and Rajagopal 2018).

Inclusivity in Business

An inclusive business model seeks to create value for low-income communities through social- or profit-based business projects that integrate the business activities into the value chain of a company. The inclusive businesses build strategic relationship with the stakeholders and key partners, and engage them in business planning, strategy development, implementation, and performance evaluation in a sustainable way. Inclusive businesses face challenging circumstances in low-income markets, which may influence the configuration of the business model in the context of the socio-economic attributes of the ecosystem at the BOP. However, the lack of formal market institutions in low-income markets causes uncertain demand, high transaction costs, low purchasing power, and cannibalization by the local brands. Consequently, firm aiming to work with inclusive businesses to serve the customers at the BOP needs to look at alternative ways to lower the transaction costs and empower stakeholders in marketing process. Unilever's social strategy of empowering rural women through the *Shakti* program (*Shakti* meaning Power in Hindi language) to create brand awareness and community marketing, and support economic well-being at the household level in India, which has created enormous customer value and sustainable behavior. *Project Shakti* enables rural women in villages across India in inculcating an entrepreneurial mindset and helps them become financially independent marketers of HUL products. To provide regular income, these women entrepreneurs are trained on the basic principles of distribution management and familiarization with the company's products. In this process, rural sales promoters coach women by familiarizing them with HUL products to manage their businesses better. Imparting such training in women entrepreneurs develops soft skills of negotiation and communication and prepares them as business associates of the company. This strategy of empowering rural women to expand the market horizon of

HUL is consistent with the elements of the design cube. Shakti project was a win-win initiative taken by HUL to conquer the universe of market (premium, upper mass, economic mass, lower mass, and BOP). The bottom-of-the-market was aimed to be covered through the Shakti project. The broad task of the project was to promote sales and distribution of HUL products through several embedded initiatives. The Shakti initiative of HUL is a perfect blend of performance with purpose by creating social values, corporate values, and market values simultaneously. This experiment was a good fit to the design cube concept as it explains all the three facets of the cube comprising design-to-market, design-to-society, and design-to-value (Rajagopal 2021a).

One way to work with the inclusive business is fully engaging the stakeholders, which helps to design the business model in the local context, as firms often encourage internalizing solutions for local market to expand the business and enhance outreach of customers. However, such business models are expensive due to high transaction costs, investment in customer relationship, and voluminous sales promotions. Improving the business ecosystem around inclusive business models can help firms overcome the social market gaps and implement business models with high-touch, high-cost, and often small-scale while positioning the ethnic products in the upstream markets. Such brands or products can be marketing with an inclusive history of the product. For example, organic fashion apparel is being sold at the upstream market for premium consumers by tagging the storyboard of inclusive manufacturing process. An agile business model can adjust both internal and external needs and respond to the changes in the business ecosystems. However, a robust business model focuses on adjusting to the external fit and improves the organizational capabilities and competencies to achieve win-win goals within the business ecosystem. The robust strategic business model can be created through an effective business model that stands as foolproof against the external changes, while the other way is to build a business model by operating in a local business ecosystem that is sheltered in a niche avoiding the impact of external factors (Danse et al. 2020). The attributes and challenges of inclusive businesses are illustrated in Figure 1.3.

Inclusivity in business is largely driven by the corporate and social dynamics in the firms to build value-driven business organization as

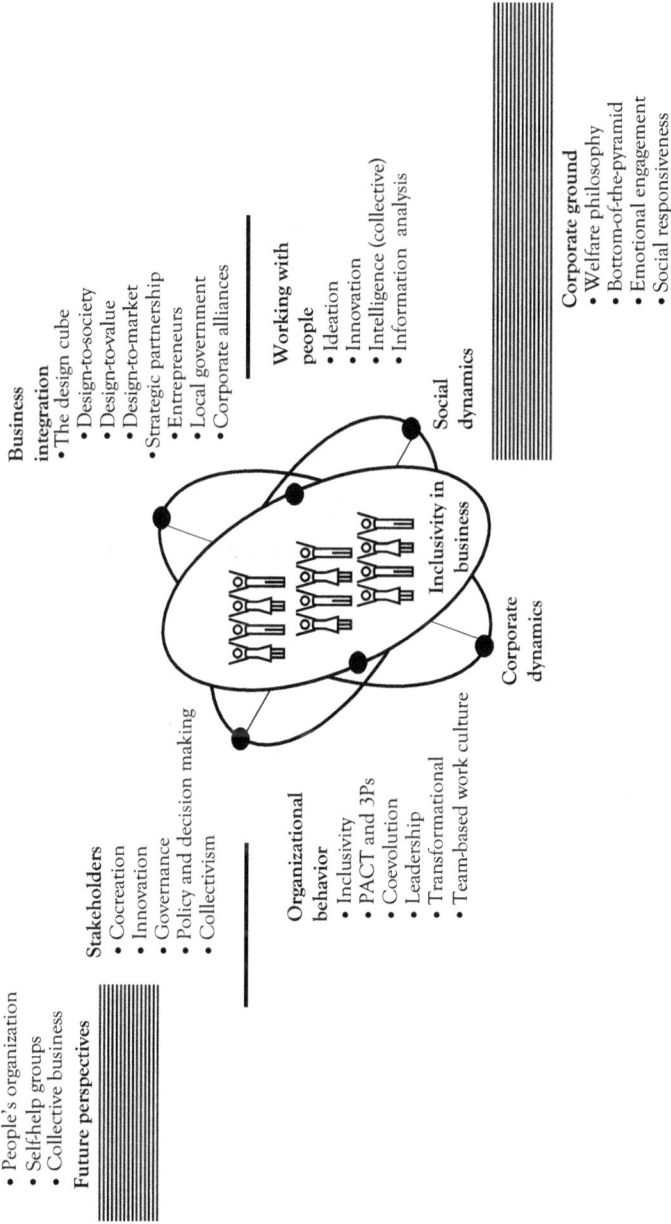

Figure 1.3 Inclusivity in business

Source: Author

exhibited in Figure 1.3. The corporate dynamics help firms to embed stakeholders in innovation, governance, policy making, and cocreation by inculcating collectivism as organizational philosophy. Such stakeholder inclusiveness would lead firms to experience changes in organizational behavior and encourage practices to comply with the triple bottom line philosophy and PACT approach to coevolve business. The inclusivity approach in business largely promotes team-based work culture and transformational leadership. The social dynamics demand firms to develop businesses by reorienting their philosophy toward design-to-society and design-to-value and develop strategic partnership and corporate alliance with the local bodies to coevolve business.

An inclusive business framework with integration of business canvas elements allows designing, describing, categorizing, and analyzing the strategic perspectives of inclusive business model irrespective of hierarchical decision making, value-chain attributes, and proprietary rules and leverages of the size of the company. Research on the inclusiveness in business model with a focus on BOP indicates that the inclusivity helps companies to take generic decisions in the context of PNS factors. The business models with inclusiveness encompass the following elements (Morris et al. 2005):

- Customized or standardized value proposition;
- Balancing the internal and external factors in manufacturing and marketing;
- Developing business models in the context of industrial marketing (business-to-business), consumer marketing (business-to consumer), network marketing (customer-to-customer through social media channels), and hybrid marketing (online-to-offline channel convergence);
- Competitive marketing strategy in the context of quality deployment, marketing cost, innovation leadership; and customer relationship;
- Managing economic factors including key partners, key resources, pricing, and revenue streams.

Companies following design-to-society and design-to-value philosophy in business largely adhere to the inclusivity practices in managing business by connecting with the employees and stakeholders. Such corporate behavior leads to employee engagement and stakeholder engagement, which strengthen the corporate management practices of inclusiveness in business (Kennedy and Link 2019). Inclusivity in business has been planned in a novel way by an Indian hotel company Lemon Tree, which employs large numbers of people with disabilities and other socially marginalized groups including orphans, divorcees, widows, and members of the transgender community. The company has adopted such charitable endeavor, and this unusual human-resources strategy (inclusion program) has evolved and is now an integral part of the business model and a source of competitive advantage (Wernick and Upadhyay 2021). Inclusive business in developing countries is growing increasingly profitable by operating on digital platforms, which has encouraged firms to cocreate mainstream innovations. These companies are based on the collective intelligence and social conscious learning that has significantly pushed the inclusive venturing capabilities. Such firms are being leveraged to explore inclusive business strategically and invest more systematically within the ecosystem business models. Inclusive businesses are maturing in the farm and nonfarm sector businesses with the growing support of public policies, and supply chain and payments infrastructure. These firms as emerging companies are purpose-built to serve design engaging people at the BOP. Inclusive business relationships demonstrate the following attributes:

- Building cooperation between all players in the chain with a common goal;
- Developing new relations to strengthen collective strategies, participatory marketing, and cocreated supply value management;
- Cocreating a fair and transparent policy of open communication, fair prices, and risk sharing;
- Ensuring equal access to credit, technology, market information, and so on;
- Developing inclusive innovation; and
- Encouraging reverse accountability toward implementation, monitoring, and evaluation of marketing and communication strategies.

For example, four vegetable farmers' cooperatives in Jinotega, Nicaragua, started providing safe, high-quality vegetables to national Subway outlets in 2016. These cooperatives have devised an inclusive business model, which focuses on long-term commitments from both parties, stable and fair prices for the farmers, and a reliable supply of quality vegetables, to the Subway. The interorganization collaboration between cooperatives and Subway has opened many doors for vegetable farming in Nicaragua. Working as an alliance, the four cooperatives have managed to cross the threshold of the informal market and sell to formal markets.[1]

Organizations managing inclusive businesses invest in developing partnerships that have tangible benefits for both firms and stakeholders. These companies continuously explore new ways of reaching people at the BOP. Such win-win partnerships are more likely to help in managing inclusive businesses. The alliance-based inclusive businesses plan for scaling (economy of scale) their business models with a focus on financial sustainability and long-term impact. Firms operating with inclusive business philosophy tend to minimize delivery costs, and maximize delivery and access to their products and services. These firms outreach customers through technology and lean staffing. Several companies face challenges in searching talent and improving skills by making significant investments in training to improve the productivity, distribution, and marketing operations. The continuous learning and inclusivity in business are focused at the BOP social segment. Companies with these attributes are engaged in developing low-cost innovative products and services that can improve the conscious consumption, social value, and lifestyle (IFC 2016). *Bkash*,[2] a microfinance company of Bangladesh, has built partnerships with multiple mobile network operators rather than a single company to make mobile financial services available to

---

[1] For details, see Rikolto International S.O.N., Blijde Inkomststraat 50, BE-3000 Leuven, Belgium (www.rikolto.org).

[2] Bkash is a private limited company created specifically to provide mobile financial services in Bangladesh. It is part of the BRAC group, a nongovernment organization (NGO) that provides social services within the country.

millions of people at the BOP in the country. This company leveraged a network of the existing commercial distributors in lieu of building an expensive distribution network. *Bkash* invests in organizational capacity building by offering training to microentrepreneurs and encourages them to register and support stakeholders. Equipping these entrepreneurs with anti–money laundering, fraud management, and other financial protection knowledge, the company intends to create social value and inclusive services within the microfinance industry. However, the digital financial technologies (Fintech) and digital services do not clearly ensure the financial inclusion in the rural context of Bangladesh (Aziz and Naima 2021). Broad digitization can also broaden the access to loans and financing through Fintech applications, cryptocurrency, and other innovative forms of alternative finance.

The diffusion of business knowledge, analytical skills to determine the PNS factors, and setting up the collectivistic principles in ideation, innovation, intelligence, and information streamlining (4Is) constitutes the important factors for the team stability. Convergence among the above-discussed entrepreneurial factors plays an effective moderating role of team collectivism and dynamics (Agarwal et al. 2016). Although organizational culture is an important factor that influences corporate decision-making efforts and the ensuing corporate behavior, the inclusivity in business helps in the convergence of social values and governance. Such corporate philosophy in developing countries is meaningful and makes significant differences in motivating stakeholder investment and governance in inclusive businesses. The inclusivity in business needs strong relations between the degree of personal attitude of managers, stakeholder engagement, and relative public-private investment in developing countries (Graham et al. 2013). Inclusiveness in the telecommunication industry has promoted extensive outreach of mobile phones at the BOP consumer segment through its inclusive business model. The Reliance Telecom Company in India has expanded the range of phones to in alliance with Google to manufacture affordable 4G handsets for the consumers at the BOP. The company also aims at expanding the telecommunication network to 5G in 2030s and provides broadband Internet to millions of people in the rural areas.

Cutting Edge in Business

Innovation has emerged as a true engine of business growth for the companies after human capital (Kotsopoulos et al. 2021). Innovative differentiation in the marketplace is brought to the markets by "start-up or seed companies" across the world, as it is evidenced by the big emerging markets like China and India in reference to the local growth and business dynamics. To maximize the business performance, companies should ensure that the key enablers of entrepreneurship and innovation including managerial skills, capital, infrastructure, and research and development are applied to drive innovation. The innovation-driven companies should also overcome the challenges associated with asymmetric product demand and the changing consumer preferences. In short, innovation in a company needs to underpin any change faster than the competitors. Boosting innovation-led business performance largely depends on how quickly the company can move to competitive production that focuses on innovation- and technology-driven products. Most companies are continuously engaged in bringing consumer innovations to the market diffusing new insights among the market players to create quick impacts of competitive differentiations among the consumers. Gaining access to and deploying these innovations easily and cost-effectively in the market drives the success of companies today. The new technology trends in the 21st century affect the innovation process of consumer-centric and business-to-business-oriented companies.

Most of the innovations triggered by the start-up enterprises are woven around the needs and preferences of consumer toward convenience, sustainable technology, and value for money bargain. Such product innovations include technology-driven products for the mass consumers. Robotic technology with easy-to-use baby products, such as a baby seat that bounces and sways like human parents, has emerged as a crash performer in the USA, while some innovations are also marketed for meeting social responsibility. For example, an emerging company Boll and Branch in Chatham, NJ, has developed organic, fair-trade, and direct-to-consumer bedding, and dedicated a portion of the revenue earned from the sales of this project to "Not for Sale," an antihuman-trafficking organization. Another innovation in consumer foods is about nongenetically modified food carried out in a nonconventional way. An engineer by training, who spent months perfecting the recipe for coconut chips, which he needed for his mother's Thai lettuce wraps, worked on innovative coconut chips with five flavors from Salted Caramel to Original. He developed a family business to export his innovative snacks from Thailand. In 2014, his products have won "The Best Snack Award" in the Fancy Foods show in the United States, and in 2012, the entrepreneur built a non-GMO certified company known as Dang Foods in Berkley, CA, with the exclusivity of his innovation. Such business projects originate from the start-ups and evolve to a larger scale, provided the innovations are nurtured properly during the business evolution process.

The expansion of ecological innovation has been accompanied by the philosophy of in-home solutions with low-cost technologies and high-utilitarian values. Considering the growing global environmental concerns, such as green energy and the increasing scarcity of resources, the manufacturing industries have shown more interest in sustainable production with the social business models. These models present the low-end economic benefits for the consumers and are jointly implemented through the public-private partnership as corporate social responsibility (CSR) initiatives. However, the social awareness and effective implementation of public policies have improved the efficiency of sustainable consumption and growth of the emerging markets. Reduction in the emission of greenhouse gases has been considered as priority among the governments of developing countries, and many have adopted strategic frameworks. Interestingly, the economic leverage to enterprises engaged in manufacturing green products and providing eco-conservation services, developing countries have raised social consciousness from the environmental protection programs to achieve sustainable goals. In developing countries, the green recovery public policy has attracted public investment in environmental technologies and encouraged the implementation of collaborative sustainability projects. Green recovery projects are targeted toward regenerating ecological conservation that have been affected by the community ignorance in urban-rural geodemographic segments (Rajagopal 2021). The green recovery concept has geared-up over time as a core part of economic stimulus measures at global–local levels.

Case Studies

Anand Milk Union Limited (Amul), India

The White Revolution in India has empowered dairy farmers during the early fifties in the 20th century and guided them to organize as a cooperative institution to strengthen their economic bargaining power against the local business exploitation. Amul, which was established in 1946 in the state of Gujarat in the western part India as a Kaira District cooperative milk producers' union, has grown today as the largest dairy cooperative group in India. The sales turnover, milk procurement, and producer members have continuously increased and boomed after the mid-2000s contributing significantly to the economic growth of the country. Amul procures a daily average of 23 million liters of milk from producers in village dairy cooperative societies, and its sales turnover in the year 2019 through 2020 was INR 385 billion. Amul business model is a clear example of inclusive business, which has empowered stakeholder in dairy cooperatives in India. This business model emphasizes collection of milk from numerous small-scale producers and selling liquid milk and dairy products in the nationwide market. Amul has been supported with a wide distribution network by the key partner Gujarat Cooperative Milk Marketing Federation (GCMMF) within with cooperative consortium, which provides an established system of distribution and sales of the products of milk-producing cooperatives within the country (Shimokado 2021). In addition, by becoming a channel leader in dairy distribution, Amul has established the system that returns most of the sales profits to the following cooperative institutions:

- The members of village Dairy Cooperative Society (DCS);
- Affiliated district Cooperative Milk Producers' Unions that process liquid milk and dairy products and provide support programs to producers; and
- GCMMF as a marketing organization for Amul and affiliated cooperatives that manufacture milk products.

Amul has expanded its business alliance with the provincial dairy cooperatives and sought the government support to link the local cooperative institutions. The milk sector in Maharashtra, a western province in India, is dominated by co-operatives in various agribusiness sectors and dairy cooperative society in each district. However, many cooperatives doing business independently are causing marketing complexities due to cannibalization of market share. *Aarey*, the state government's brand, and Mahananda, the brand of the milk cooperatives apex body, also compete with the private dairies in this space. The milk industry in the state is organized in three segments: government, cooperative, and private. It has been observed in various research studies that even the private dairies in the country suffer from inadequate infrastructure and financial shape. To ease the market complexities, Amul had sourced milk from the cooperative sector despite itself being a cooperative.

However, despite the success of Amul, the competitive threat from multinationals like Nestlé and Unilever, who are competing fiercely with Amul in value-added products like yogurt and cheese, is increasing. However, the market share of Amul has been divided with the entry of large multibrand retailers like Walmart and Carrefour in the Indian market. The increasing market competition has developed the low-cost distribution network to stay price-competitive and increase the outreach to customers. The dairy farmers of Amul and affiliated cooperatives have often been politicized in the interest of local national political gains which often compromise the functionality and philosophy of cooperatives (Deshpande et al. 2013).

Amul Dairy has diversified its portfolio of dairy products to stay competitive in the consumer market segment. The cooperative has set several progressive initiatives and responded to health-conscious consumer trends with continuous product development. Camel milk, a relatively new health-oriented dairy product, is being hailed as white gold in Australia, and Middle Eastern and Western countries. Amul Dairy had an opportunity in 2015 to take advantage of the changing consumer preferences and move ahead in the growing dairy market by launching the sale of camel milk in India. Despite the major challenge of short shelf-life, Amul has launched the Camel milk in India as a source of natural insulin and protein (Puri et al. 2016). This product is posturized and marketed in two presentations. In addition, Amul has a wide product line in the portfolio of cow's milk. Amul also produces and markets buffalo's milk in Indian market. By virtue of this powerful nationwide marketing network and inclusive business model, Amul has realized long-term growth by managing its product portfolios. Its growth has resulted in sustainable development of both the economy and the local communities, and significantly enhanced the management capability and skills of its members (Shimokado 2021).

Grameen Bank, Bangladesh

The success of the *Grameen Bank* of Bangladesh as a bank for the poor is because of its niche operations as well as extensive outreach to women. The vision and goal of this bank are to engage stakeholders in farm and nonfarm financial management and provide sustainable benefits to the borrowers within the community by reducing the incidence of poverty. The concept and institution of the Grameen Bank has been founded by Dr. Muhammad Yunus (an innovative economics professor and a Nobel Peace Prize winner) with a highly decentralized management structure engaging the stakeholders to provide financial services for community development and improving the quality of life. Dr. Yunus and his colleagues at Chittagong University of Bangladesh, conscious of the general conditions of poverty in the villages around the Chittagong campus, initiated an experimental project in a nearby village in 1976. This institution is based on the collective management maxim with a focus on people, accountability, community control, and transformational leadership (PACT). Though this microfinancial institution is supported by the subsidized funds and grants, it has the potential capacity to operate with collective resources. On the other hand, Grameen Bank has a high credit recovery rate and a positive impact on rural wages. Consequently, the benefits from the participation and contributions of stakeholders have resulted into highly sustainable operations of the bank within the country (Khandekar 1994).

The Grameen Bank model of microcredit has a unique set of social objectives besides providing financial resources through microcredit policies to the people at the BOP. It also aims at holistically improving the social values and quality of life at the grassroots of the society. The broad philosophy of the bank embeds promotion of credit for economic development of the stakeholder as a human right, particularly for the poor women. The operational success of the bank is based on mutual trust instead of legal procedures and system. The purpose of institutional credit is to create self-employment, income-generating activities, and housing for the poor, unlike using the community financial resources for consumption purpose. It was initiated as a challenge to conventional banking which rejected the poor by classifying them as not creditworthy due to the absence of adequate collateral security. This bank, with its inclusive business philosophy, has emerged as an institution, which provides services at the doorstep by reaching out to the poor. It gives high priority to building social capital and marginal profit with a purpose to be redistributed as dividend among the stakeholders. Over the years, the Grameen Bank has become a global symbol of poor women's empowerment and is celebrated for its 98 percent loan recovery (Karim 2008).

The Grameen Bank's organizational structure is divided into four administrative levels comprising branch, area, zone, and head office. As the foundation of the structure, a branch employs 10 people and serves approximately 50 to 60 groups of five members each constituting the microcredit communities. The bank operates with blocks of 10 to 15 branches, which are supervised by an area office and, in turn, about 14 area offices are looked after by a zonal or regional office. The bank administration encourages all employees to finish an intensive 12-month training program covering the areas of computerization, accounts, administration, leadership, crisis management, community values, and social development perspectives. Nonetheless, employees are encouraged to inculcate the learning-by-doing behavior. Such an open community-led services ecosystem promotes the innovative ideas within the institution.

The Grameen Bank has emerged as a marketing-oriented financial organization over time with social objective to target a homogeneous group of rural poor. Many stakeholders of the organization feel comfortable with small investment in small businesses or entrepreneurial activities such as small-scale poultry farming, producing puffed rice, making bamboo furniture, weaving floor mats with jute and palm leaves, and paddy husking. The microcredit programs of the bank have been designed to fit the needs of stakeholders to promote the productive use of community credit with less formal paperwork. The needs-focused program and personal attention have been the key service objectives of the bank. Besides community development objectives, the social reforms-oriented movement of the bank includes reducing the influence of local moneylenders. The bank provides easy repayment schedule, and the principal along with the associated interest is collected in weekly instalments. As a part of the stakeholder services, the bank provides an intensive service to borrowers such as investment advice, and training in accounting and management to inculcate the sense of productive use of credit for personal and social development.

Unlike collateral-based lending operations, the Grameen Bank evaluates the proposed projects on the basis of the merit of productive utilization of resources and its possible impact on the household income. Accordingly, the decision on making the credit available is made based on group credit worthiness. The borrowers are required to form a group of five coborrowers to invest the capital resources in an enterprise (manufacturing or services). However, before the formation of a group, its members are offered a comprehensive training session by the bank to acquaint them with the policies of the bank. Such training is based on adult education objectives that encompass developing basic skills in the stakeholders on basic reading and signing the documents and making key decisions. Each group elects a chairperson and a secretary to ensure participation by all group members at core meetings. Evidence shows that the bank successfully targets poor women and offers them the opportunity to improve their quality of life by implementing inclusive business model (Wahid and Hsu 2000).

References

Agarwal, R., B.A. Campbell, A.M. Franco, and M. Ganco. 2016. "What Do I Take With Me? The Mediating Effect of Spin-Out Team Size and Tenure on the Founder–Firm Performance Relationship." *Academy of Management Journal* 59, no. 3, pp. 1060–1087.

Aziz, A., and U. Naima. 2021. "Rethinking Digital Financial Inclusion: Evidence From Bangladesh." *Technology in Society*, p. 64. (in press). https://doi .org/10.1016/j.techsoc.2020.101509.

Balakrishnan, J., P. Foroudi, and Y.K. Dwivedi. 2020. "Does Online Retail Coupons and Memberships Create Favorable Psychological Disposition?" *Journal of Business Research* 116, no. 2, pp. 229–244.

Bhattacharya, A.K., and D.C. Michael. 2008. "How Local Companies Keep Multinationals at Bay." Harvard Business Review.

Carmona-Lavado, A., G. Cuevas-Rodríguez, and C. Cabello-Medina. 2013. "Service Innovativeness and Innovation Success in Technology-based Knowledge-Intensive Business Services: An Intellectual Capital Approach." *Industry and Innovation* 20, no. 2, pp. 133–156.

Chen, A., Y. Lu, and B. Wang. 2017. "Customers' Purchase Decision-Making Process in Social Commerce: A Social Learning Perspective." *International Journal of Information Management* 37, no. 6, pp. 627–638.

Dann, J.B., K. Bennett, and A. Ogden. 2017. *Xiaomi: Designing an Ecosystem For the Internet of Things.* Greif Center for Entrepreneurial Studies, Marshall School of Business, Los Angeles, CA: University of Southern California.

Danse, M., L. Klerkx, J. Reintjes, R. Rabbinge, and C. Leeuwis. 2020. "Unravelling Inclusive Business Models for Achieving Food and Nutrition Security in BOP Markets." *Global Food Security*, p. 24. (in press). https://doi .org/10.1016/j.gfs.2020.100354.

Deshpande, R., T. Khanna, N. Arora, and T. Bijlani. 2013. *India's Amul: Keeping Up with the Times.* Cambridge: Harvard Business School Press.

Edelman, D.C., and M. Singer. 2015. "Competing on Customer Journeys." Harvard Business Review.

Graham, J.R., C.R. Harvey, and M. Puri. 2013. "Managerial Attitudes and Corporate Actions." *Journal of Financial Economics* 109, pp. 103–121.

Grewal, D., A.L. Roggeveen, and J. Nordfält. 2017. "The Future of Retailing." *Journal of Retailing* 93, no. 1, pp. 1–6.

Hein, A., M. Schreieck, T. Riasanow, D.S. Setzke, M. Wiesche, M. Böhm, and H. Krcmar. 2020. "Digital Platform Ecosystems." *Electronic Markets* 30, no. 1, pp. 87–98.

IFC. 2016. *Inclusive Business Models International Finance Corporation.* Washington, DC: International Finance Corporation.

Karim, L. 2008. "Demystifying Micro-Credit: The Grameen Bank, NGOs, and Neoliberalism in Bangladesh." *Cultural Dynamics* 20, no. 1, pp. 5–29.

Kennedy, J.T., and P.J. Link. 2019. *Companies Need to Do More for Employees and Customers With Disabilities.* Harvard Business Review Digital Article, Cambridge, MA: Harvard Business School Press.

Khachatryan, H., A. Rihn, B. Behe, C. Hall, B. Campbell, J. Dennis, and C. Yue. 2018. "Visual Attention, Buying Impulsiveness, and Consumer Behavior." *Marketing Letters* 29, no. 1, pp. 23–35.

Khakimdjanova, L., and J. Park. 2005. "Online Visual Merchandising Practice of Apparel E-Merchants." *Journal of Retailing and Consumer Services* 12, no. 5, pp. 307–318.

Khandker, S., B. Khalily, and Z. Khan. 1994. *Is Grameen Bank Sustainable?* Human Resources Development and Operations Policy Working Paper # 23. Washington DC: World Bank.

Kim, H.Y., J.Y. Lee, J.M. Mun, and K.K. Johnson. 2016. "Consumer Adoption of Smart In-Store Technology: Assessing the Predictive Value of Attitude Versus Beliefs in the Technology Acceptance Model." *International Journal of Fashion Design, Technology and Education* 10, no. 1, pp. 26–36.

Kotsopoulos, D., A. Karagianaki, and S. Baloutsos. 2021. "The Effect of Human Capital, Innovation Capacity, and Covid-19 Crisis on Knowledge-Intensive Enterprises' Growth Within a VC-Driven Innovation Ecosystem." *Journal of Business Research* 139, pp. 1177–1191.

Lamberton, C., and A.T. Stephen. 2016. "A Thematic Exploration of Digital, Social Media, and Mobile Marketing: Rresearch Evolution From 2000 to 2015 and an Agenda for Future Inquiry." *Journal of Marketing* 80, no. 6, pp. 146–172.

Laursen, K., and A. Salter. 2006. "Open for Innovation: The Role of Openness in Explaining Innovation Performance Among UK Manufacturing Firms." *Strategic Management Journal* 27, no. 2, pp. 131–150.

Leung, X., L. Xue, and H. Wen. 2019. "Framing the Sharing Economy: Toward a Sustainable Ecosystem." *Tourism Management* 71, no. 1, pp. 44–53.

Li, Y.M., J.H. Liou, and C.Y. Ni. 2019. "Diffusing Mobile Coupons With Social Endorsing Mechanism." *Decision Support Systems* 117, no. 1, pp. 87–99.

Lo, L.Y.S., S.W. Lin, and L.Y. Hsu. 2016. "Motivation for Online Impulse Buying: A Two-Factor Theory Perspective." *International Journal of Information Management* 36, no. 5, pp. 759–772.

Martín, M.V., R. Reinhardt, and S. Gurtner. 2021. "The Dilemma of Downstream Market Stakeholder Involvement in NPD: Untangling the Effects of Involvement and Capabilities on Performance." *Journal of Business Research* 124, pp. 136–151.

Morris, M., M. Schindehutte, and J. Allen. 2005. "The Entrepreneur's Business Model: Toward a Unified Perspective." *Journal of Business Research*, no. 58, pp. 726–735.

Mudambi, S.M., and D. Schuff. 2010. "What Makes a Helpful Review? A Study of Customer Reviews on Amazon.com." *MIS Quarterly* 34, no. 1, pp. 185–200.

Neeley, S. 2005. "Influences on Consumer Socialisation." *Young Consumers* 6, no. 2, pp. 63–69.

Olson, E.M., K.M. Olson, A.J. Czaplewski, and T.M. Key. 2021. "Business Strategy and the Management of Digital Marketing." *Business Horizons* 64, no. 2, pp. 285–293.

Pantano, E., and M. Viassone. 2014. "Demand Pull and Technology Push Perspective in Technology-Based Innovations for the Points of Sale: The Retailers' Evaluation." *Journal of Retailing and Consumer Services* 21, no. 1, pp. 43–47.

Park, J., J.N. Lee, O.K.D. Lee, and Y. Koo. 2017. "Alignment Between Internal and External IT Governance and Its Effects on Distinctive Firm Performance: An Extended Resource-Based View." *IEEE Transactions on Engineering Management* 64, no. 3, pp. 351–364.

Puri, S., B.M. Taneja, P. Gupta, and A. Menon. 2016. *Amul Dairy: Camel Milk Launch in India.* Cambridge, MA: Harvard Business School Press.

Rajagopal. 2020. *Market Entropy: How to Manage Chaos and Uncertainty for Improving Organizational Performance.* New York, NY: Business Expert Press.

Rajagopal. 2021. *Sustainable Businesses in Developing Economies—Socio-Economic and Governance Perspectives.* New York, NY: Palgrave Macmillan.

Rajagopal. 2021a. *The Business Design Cube: Converging Markets, Society, and Customer Values to Grow Competitive in Business.* New York, NY: Business Expert Press.

Rajagopal and A. Rajagopal. 2018. "Brand Literacy and Knowledge Transfer Process: Analysis of Purchase Intentions Among Consumers in Mexico." *International Journal of Business Innovation and Research* 16, no. 3, pp. 302–323.

Rong, K., B. Li, W. Peng, D. Zhou, and X. Shi. 2021. "Sharing Economy Platforms: Creating Shared Value at a Business Ecosystem Level." *Technological Forecasting and Social Change*, p. 169. (in press). https://doi.org/10.1016/j.techfore.2021.120804.

Salgado, M., and J.B. Clempner. 2018. "Measuring the Emotional State Among Interacting Agents: A Game Theory Approach Using Reinforcement Learning." *Expert Systems With Applications* 97, no. 2, pp. 266–275.

Shimokado, N. 2021. "Inclusive Business and Sustainable Rural Development in India: A Case Study of the AMUL Community-Based Food Chain." In H. Shioji, D.R. Adhikari, F. Yoshino, and T. Hayashi (eds), *Management for Sustainable and Inclusive Development in a Transforming Asia*, pp. 59–71, Singapore: Springer.

Shin, D., J. Jung, and B. Chang. 2012. "The Psychology Behind QR Codes: User Experience Perspective." *Computers in Human Behavior* 28, pp. 1417–1426.

Steinhoff, L., D. Arli, S. Weaven, and I.V. Kozlenkova. 2019. "Online Relationship Marketing." *Journal of Academy of Marketing Science* 47, no. 3, pp. 369–393.

Sun, J., S. Wu, and K. Yang. 2018. "An Ecosystemic Framework for Business Sustainability." *Business Horizons* 61, no. 1, pp. 59–72.

Van Alstyne, M.W., G. Parker, and S.P. Choudary. 2016. "Pipelines, Platforms, and the New Rules of Strategy." Harvard Business Review.

Verhagen, T., and W. van Dolen. 2011. "The Influence of Online Store Beliefs on Consumer Online Impulse Buying: A Model and Empirical Application." *Information & Management* 48, pp. 320–327.

Visnjic, I., A. Neely, C. Cennamo, and N. Visnjic. 2016. "Governing the City: Unleashing Value From the Business Ecosystem." *California Management Review* 59, no. 1, pp. 109–140.

Wahid, A., and M. Hsu. 2000. "The Grameen Bank of Bangladesh: History Procedures, Effects and Challenges." *Asian Affairs* 31, no. 2, pp. 160–169.

Wei, Z., X. Song, and D. Wang. 2017. "Manufacturing Flexibility, Business Model Design, and Firm Performance." *International Journal of Production and Economics* 193, no. 1, pp. 87–97.

Wernick, D.A., and S.K. Upadhyay. 2021. *Does the U.S. Hospitality Market Offer Fertile Soil for Lemon Tree Hotels' Inclusive Business Model?* Cambridge, MA: Harvard Business School Press.

Williamson, P., and A. De Meyer. 2022. *How to Monetize a Business Ecosystem.* Harvard Business Review Digital Article. Cambridge, MA: Harvard Business School Press.

Yi, Y., Y. Chen, and D. Li. 2022. "Stakeholder Ties, Organizational Learning, and Business Model Innovation: A Business Ecosystem Perspective." *Technovation* 114. (in press). https://doi.org/10.1016/j.technovation.2021.102445.

CHAPTER 2

Inclusive Business Design

This chapter discusses the process of inclusive business design by converging the stakeholders in the BOP. This chapter argues that considering the consumer behavior and attributes of market players in the BOP market segment, there is still need for the firms to keep exploring the ways to effectively reach people and create value. This section also reviews the previous research contributions of C. K. Prahalad and Garry Hammel on the BOP concept to discuss inclusive business modeling process. In addition, this chapter also focuses on crowd behavior, consumer preferences, and associated values (customer and social), and explains the need for thinking out of the box to explore cocreation and coevolution prospects. Contextual to inclusive business strategies, this chapter argues that cocreation is a phenomenon that helps companies in providing tailored services and higher customer satisfaction to manage business in the emerging markets. This chapter also discusses crowd-based business modeling, shared economy, and inclusivity. The discussion on social engagement and coevolution of business is also central to this chapter. The concepts of inclusivity, cocreation, and coevolution in social enterprises have been illustrated through the case studies on energy cooperatives in the Netherlands and Probiotech Agribusiness in Nepal.

Stakeholders, Inclusivity, and Collectivism in Business

The concept of inclusive business is contextual to the socio-economic performance, public policy, and corporate socio-ethical values. Inclusive business companies adapt to social business practices by invoking the concept of value or virtue that considers freedom and justice, and societal, political, and economic solidarity. Such business models emphasize inclusion of the poor in business to incite the economic and moral aspects of business performance (Stainer and Stainer 1998). With the paucity of public development finance in many developing countries, investments in public infrastructure and social development have been scaled down. However, with the increasing response to free market reforms, governments of developing countries have encouraged the private sector to bring new investment for the economic growth in semiurban and rural areas. The foundations laid by business climate initiatives, investment promotion in social development, and market-based entrepreneurial push have served as powerful enablers of inclusive businesses (German et al. 2020). Consequently, inclusivity in business has emerged as design-to-society business model to enhance the compatibility between local business and corporate expansion. The underlying philosophy of inclusive business has been actively supported by governments, NGOs, and leading agri-food and customer-centric companies such as Nestlé (enabling technology and training to the coffee growers), Unilever (empowering women in developing countries), Google (information outreach to remote areas), Levy Strauss & Co. (diverse and inclusive workplace), and Starbucks (coffee and farmers equity). Besides the social engagement of large companies, inclusive business is also promoted among the small and medium enterprises through business alliances with local firms and cooperatives. Such business models have benefitted the stakeholders and people by integrating them into business value-chains (in the farm and nonfarm sector) in developing economies (Chamberlain and Anseeuw 2019).

Inclusive businesses are growing selectively across industries and destinations despite most companies addressing the customer needs amid the rising complexities of competition in the market. Darwinism can be well explained in the global business scenarios, as multinational companies are exploring remote markets, while the hatched niche markets are seeking a way out to wider congregations. In this business dynamics, success is not guaranteed to the companies irrespective of their size, resources, and power. On reviewing several attributes of business today, few questions often arise such as why businesses fail and does design matter. SMART (strategic, measurable, accessible, responsive, and trustworthy) and socially connected business designs raise a broad set of new strategic choices converging the attributes of markets, social responsiveness, and customer values to help companies perform as a corporate citizen (Rajagopal 2021). By creating social and customer values, and securing competitive advantage by acquiring new capabilities to reshape, industries are experiencing increasing challenges for companies in emerging markets.

The concept of BOP introduced by Prahalad, Hammel, and Hammond in the 1990s has motivated several new business initiatives, development institution programs, and innovative investment funds that focused on doing business at the bottom-line market segment. Most multinational companies have moved today to the remotest marketplaces to do business by engaging customers to cocreate products and markets. The concept of bottom-of-the pyramid has been emerged as a new, enterprise-based approach to conduct business with people and alleviate poverty by empowering them to access global brands (Prahalad and Hammond 2002). Over time, this new lexicon was raised to describe this phenomenon, including phrases like inclusive business, subsistence marketplaces, frugal innovation, and impact investment. Some companies such as Nestlé, Kellogg's, and AMUL (India) have integrated all the above phrases into their business model, and these companies are growing today involving people with distinctive identity. However, relevant epistemologies and business research have not advanced at the same pace with the inclusive business revolution. Consequently, knowledge about parameters for successfully integrating business and working on inclusive business models remains ambiguous (Hart et al. 2016).

In large organizations, business design perspectives are becoming central to people including stakeholders. Several business designs have emerged over time as a collective approach in business organizations involving decision makers, employees, customers, and stakeholders. The involvement of people in business has been practiced in many companies as the crowd participation approach in design thinking, developing print and digital commercials for products and services, and in value cocreation programs. Engaging people in production and business operations has benefited organizations in updating their real-time knowledge on market and consumption needs (Kietzmann 2017). Most organizations have realized today that staying in business as learning organizations helps them grow competitively and consistently in the marketplace. Design thinking in business has been conceived as an essential tool for simplifying the business operation by interlinking the organization, society, and stakeholders, and more comprehensively humanizing the business. The extended principles of design thinking in businesses converge with the market attributes (market players, ethics, and business growth), social responsiveness (marketing with purpose), and value propositions of customers. The philosophy of inclusive business advocates the people-led win-win business model to lead the market (Desai 2014). The concept of inclusivity in businesses rose into prominence by the end of the twentieth century, as community workspaces and sharing of experience offered deep and meaningful relationships at work between customers and employees with the goal of collective psychodynamics. It allowed firms not only to understand the customer insights but also realize the power of cocreation and coevolution of business in the competitive marketplace. The inclusiveness in businesses has also supported gender equity at workplaces as women employees have been empowered socially and economically, which has built social synergy in business organizations (Livingston and Opie 2019). The integration of various elements of inclusivity with the business is exhibited in Figure 2.1.

Integrating internal and external stakeholders is one of the major challenges for the companies irrespective of the size of organization and volume of operations. Internal stakeholders encompass customers and investors, while the external stakeholders also include key partners comprising suppliers, service providers, consortium enterprises, innovators, and so on. Integrating people in business in a systematic manner drives inclusivity and leads to inclusive business modeling as illustrated in Figure 2.1. The inclusivity has three principal domains that include corporate focus on social and economic development through business, encouraging transformational leadership in the organization, and improving the stakeholder value. Most companies are engaged in holistic social development by involving people to design and implement strategies on poverty alleviation, housing development, improving public health, and public education conditions. In addition, stakeholder involvement in business also contributes to economic leverage through skill development, enhancing extension services, and improving the work efficiency of key partners. The transformational leadership in business encourages design thinking in the organization through empowerment and collective decisions by adopting a grassroots approach to social and economic development. Such leadership drive

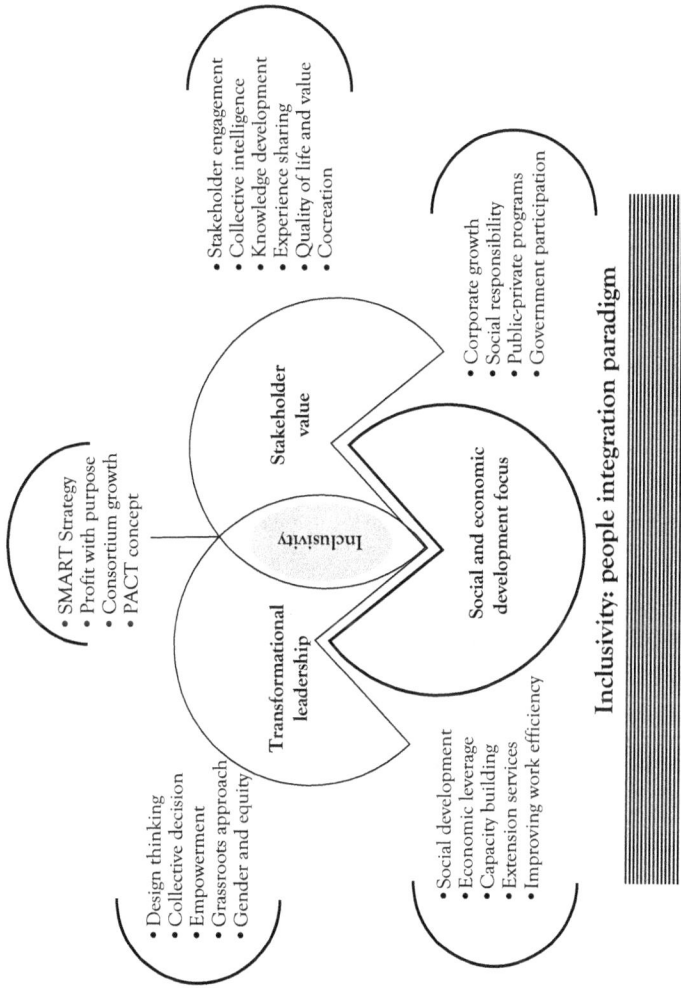

Figure 2.1 People integration paradigm of inclusive business

Source: Author

stimulates the stakeholder engagement and knowledge development. The collective intelligence helps in knowledge management through experience sharing and cocreation to improve the quality of life of both internal and external stakeholders.

Market trends and consumer behavior are continuously changing, and social media is playing a critical role in determining marketing decisions. Volatility of consumer markets can have significant, negative effects on market share, profitability, and brand equity of the companies. However, volatility is an embedded attribute of the competitive growth theory. The central argument to the theory of change management is that the companies operating in a competitive business environment consider consumer preferences, innovation, technology, and growth-related investments as dynamic variables. Customer-centric companies, therefore, tend to build simpler products to help consumers choose the right product. Involving people and engaging customers and stakeholders in the business processes transform companies as learning organizations and make them stay need-based and customer-centric in business. Inclusive businesses operate with diverse workforce and gain abilities in converging divergent business perspectives to develop a social vision for carrying out business with people. People-led firms largely support decision making, idea sharing, and emotions in managing business. Such companies develop abilities to fight conscious and unconscious biases as they coevolve with people and society (Yamkovenko and Tavares 2017). Social interactions often motivate a sustainable and social consumption of products. The interplay of consumers within the social (interpersonal) and digital (remote response) platforms also helps companies adapt to inclusive business models and stay distinctive in the competitive marketplace. Consumers today are increasingly looking for brands that have a social purpose above functional and competitive benefits. As a result, most companies are taking social stand in highly visible ways. An effective, convergent business strategy creates social and customer values by coevolving the brand in the society. The network among society, people, and business stimulates cocreation and collective business designing. This convergence of society and business can be better understood through continuous learning about the consumer behavior, operational processes, employee contributions, and competitive growth perspectives (Rajagopal 2021).

Inclusive business provides a better model for social license as people-led firms operate in a competitive marketplace. Such business approaches have gained momentum in consumer marketing segments. Inclusive businesses could bridge social needs and lead to multiple business outcomes based on *profit with purpose* goals. Many inclusive social businesses led by the technology-based companies (in agriculture, energy, and ecology management sector) have contributed to the long-term sustainability (Sawmy 2015). Value is often measured in either economic or social terms. The blended-value proposition emphasizes that true customer value, which is a blend of economic, social, and environmental components, is indivisible. After the success of networking practices of business activities with social media over decades, profit-seeking firms have laid explicit emphasis on the creation of strategic social value. This business philosophy has grown in nonprofit organizations as well. Social value is dynamic, and customer-centric companies continuously monitor the perpetual changes in social values, culture, and ethnicity. An example of inclusive business may be cited of Aravind Eye Care Systems (Aravind) in India, which began its operation through the vision centers (VC) in 2015 in rural areas. This healthcare company has involved society and people as motivators and business consultants. Each VC had three key personnel comprising coordinator, ophthalmic technician, and field worker (social inclusiveness component). The VC was equipped with basic ophthalmic equipment and Internet connectivity (Shainesh and Kulkarni 2016). Consequently, to drive businesses deep into the social environment, companies adapt to the triadic philosophy of gaining social insights, blending business values in the society, and cocreating innovative socio-business strategies. The best practices reveal that these elements boost business performance by enhancing the social values and narrowing the consumer disparities (Rajagopal 2021).

One of the essential paradoxes of crowd governance is that the social media channels simultaneously enable individual and collective decision making. The computer-aided working environment has significantly affected the collective intelligence and knowledge management processes stimulating crowd behavior (Melone 2018). Several multidisciplinary research studies have revealed that people's participation in business growth and progress stimulates crowd cognition toward creating profit with social values (Ji and Kim 2019). Public governance in business helps in creating and applying shared values, norms, rules, decisions, and programs within the social perspectives for collaborative growth. People-led governance in businesses explains how the social vigilance in business organizations helps in controlling unethical moves of the firms for profit at the cost of customers and stakeholders. People's involvement in business also benefits the multistake business model and strengthens multistakeholder mechanism in business governance by co-designing the organizational structures, processes, and principles (Shi 2021). Successful companies like Nestle, Wholefoods, and Apple bring business and society back together by creating shared and economic values. In addition, crowdsourcing, crowdfunding, social marketing, and sharing the economy platforms have been rapidly transforming the production and consumption systems in the developing economies. These platforms connect businesses with economic, social, and environmental factors across geo-demographic segments. People's participation and social governance have grown over time in promising forms of sharing and leveraging benefits to stakeholders, while circumventing its embedded problems associated with the inclusivity in business is becoming increasingly important (Mont et al. 2020).

Over the end of the twentieth century, the coffee production and marketing have experienced exceptional growth across countries in the world. However, the coffee market has grown in a complex and volatile global market environment and the economic gains in coffee-producing countries have remained largely obscure. Yet, large buyers seek to develop convergence with suppliers, investment in value-added production, and competitive leverages to create lead in the market and enhance shared value. Among many developing countries engaged in quality coffee production, Colombia is the third largest coffee producer in the Latin America, which has predominantly small-scale farmers cultivating premium-quality coffee beans in the highlands of the country. Expocafé S.A., a limited-liability private company founded by all Colombian coffee growers' cooperatives, was established in the mid-eighties. This coffee growers' company has been evolved over the years with multilayered objectives to expand its marketing operations to international buyers, attain higher scale of business, consolidate local and regional production and marketing activities, and improve agribusiness management. The effects of institutionalizing coffee growers' market were anticipated in lowering technical costs, managing risk, and overcoming the restraints of cooperatives to access global markets (McFalls 2017). Expocafé has been supported by AAA Sustainable Quality Program of Nespresso (a unit of Nestle Inc.) in Colombia to improve the production and business operations of coffee beans. Nestle began supplying coffee to Nespresso in 2002, in a run-up operation to the AAA Program.[1] The AAA Program has rolled out in phases with the principal objective of improving Nespresso's quality standard. Nespresso began to acquire coffee beans from Expocafé farmers in Caldas and engaged in exploring new flavors and aromas it wanted for its international market. With Nespresso's support, Expocafé has invested significantly in cultivating the new blend of coffee seeds. Further, in alliance with the Rainforest Alliance, an NGO, the producer cooperatives were brought into the design of the program. Under the program, agronomists and project managers were made available to the cluster of farmers at Expocafé to provide technical guidance on environmentally sustainable production methods to achieve and maintain the quality taste. The engagement with Nespresso with Expocafé had led the company to transform its key activities to a value-added services company. Consequently, the company attained new skills in the accreditation processes, and the transparent reporting of prices and margins has strengthened farmer knowledge of their worth, with it their negotiating capacity (McFalls 2017).

Customer-centric companies increasingly invest in Big Data to analyze categorical pool of data, increase organizational capabilities, and add innovative products and services in ecosystem business models. The inclusive business model helps firms in creating new possibilities to serve people's latent needs and contribute to the productivity and profit of the firm. Operating with such business model, firms can reduce costs and

---

[1] The sustainability requirements of the Nespresso AAA Sustainable Quality Program are based on social and environmental standards developed by the Sustainable Agriculture Network, a coalition of nonprofit conversation that includes the Rainforest Alliance. The AAA sustainable quality program is a registered trademark of Nestlé.

risks associated with PNS factors and gain significant market power through customers as the "gateway" for leveraging markets at the BOP. Consequently, the profitability of inclusive business is increasing, and the inclusive business model has been adopted by many leading companies such as Unilever, Danone, Mastercard, AXA, and Google. This practice has made inclusive business more relevant to every industry. The inclusive businesses stimulate cocreation, coevolution, profitability, and customer satisfaction. Some leaders are building market power and capabilities in emerging markets driven by the magnitude of the stakeholder value and loyalty. The inclusive business practice has the "transformative" potential in the medium and large firms, which significantly contributes toward augmenting social income, reduces the incidence of poverty, and narrows down societal inequalities. Many initiatives on inclusive businesses have positive response to socio-economic development and entrepreneurial business at the grassroots. For local enterprises to serve their role as development agents and invest in providing durable solutions to the poor, the objectives of inclusive business are well adapted to the business ecosystems by the firms such as *Grameen Bank* of Bangladesh (Scheyvens et al. 2016).

Crowd-Based Business Modeling

Crowd-based business model (CBBM) is characterized by integrating investors from public, who are beyond the corporate boundaries. Companies relying on CBBM tend to bring the crowd interface by exploring new technologies and developing peer-to-peer platforms and creating value to the customers and company through collective intelligence. This requires the firm to open certain resources and processes to external contributors, often resulting in a strong interaction with these contributors and their resources. The activity of these contributors can range from conducting microtasks to creating and delivering all products and services to the firm's customers. In this sense, CBBMs place even more importance on the crowd than traditional forms of crowdsourcing (Kohler 2015). Over recent years, however, firms from different industries have started to develop new business models that fundamentally integrate crowds in value-creation logic. The emergence of these crowd-based business models is both driven by advances in Internet-based technologies and a shift in the role of consumers toward becoming the so-called "prosumers" (Ritzer 2014). Crowd-based business models emerge out of the collective intelligence generated through crowdsourcing. Collective intelligence (CI)-led business models rely more on consumer preference and social criteria while evaluating the ideas that are generated through open innovation. Successful crowdsourcing ventures require more than an online platform and brand connection. Without an understanding of participant motivations and behaviors, casual attempts to leverage the wisdom of the crowd may backfire and lead to unintended results. Prominent examples of crowdsourcing failures are myriad. Consider General Motors, which provided users with web tools to make their own ads for the Chevrolet Tahoe, resulting in several viral videos that lampooned the company's products and the American automotive industry's gas guzzlers more generally. In the fast-moving consumer goods industry, Mountain Dew successfully crowdsourced part of its product development through the DEWmocracy contest series, but a similar project asking fans to name the brand's new apple-flavored drink brought on a slew of ironic suggestions, including diabetes (Fedorenko et al. 2017).

Among many consumer-centric companies, Procter & Gamble has been successfully consulting consumers into its research and development process. This company not only involves consumers and its employees in the cocreation of innovative products but also works with its superannuated employees who have specific skills. Its cocreation platform, *Connect + Develop*, has helped in continuous innovation of a variety of consumer products, boosted product development process, and effectively enhanced the participation of consumers and employees in innovation process without adding additional costs (Bughin 2014). Similarly, Heineken N. V., a Dutch brewery company, launched its cocreation platform in 2012, asking online gamers, beer drinkers, and environmentally conscious consumers to share ideas for improving its packaging to make it more sustainable. The winner, a German citizen, suggested a device (the Heineken-o-Mat) intended to turn recycling into a game. Starbucks had also called for the opinions and reviews of customers by providing a peer-interface platform for sharing views on sustainability. Interactions between companies and customers have helped in co-designing store ambiance, in-store music, and corporate social responsibility initiatives. However, using cocreation in business models and sustainability programs is often difficult for companies, as there remains a wide gap between the communication transparency and creativity in business modeling through various social and cultural approaches. Innovation in business models helps to align social and stakeholder benefits and revenue-stream management to leverage sustainable solutions (Rajagopal 2019).

Design thinking is an exercise required for developing appropriate business model based on crowdsourced ideation. Analysis of economic viability and technological feasibility of manufacturing and marketing processes defined in the CBBM is central to the innovations of targeted products within the social and market domains. The CBBM is expected to embed identification of social needs and consumption patterns in the society. Accordingly, the design-thinking process identifies the right innovation and technology needed to cocreate the second-generation products from the industrial waste, maps product attractiveness and value spread, and determines its shelf-life and end-of-the-cycle product state. The CBBM attributes broadly constitute the anticipated cost, time, and risk factors in a business operations matrix with the combination of various marketing mix elements. Industry attractiveness has always been a prerequisite for developing any type of business model. The industry attractiveness comprising new entrants, growth of substitutes, bargaining power of consumers and suppliers, and competition within the industry dominates the concerns of companies on developing appropriate marketing strategy and customer value. In an industry with fast growing competition, consumers face complexities in developing sustainable perceptions and attitude to inculcate behavior. Rapidly emerging new brands (with crowd-based ideas) from unfamiliar companies attract consumers with low prices. Although most consumers tend to experiment with low-priced products and substitute the products that deliver satisfactory experience, they fail to develop sustainable perceptions and build attitude toward repeat buying. However, industry attractiveness describes competition among traditional pipeline brands, which succeeds by optimizing the activities in their value chains. In addition, the crowdsourcing and collective intelligence have helped companies and their brand streamline with the customer perceptions, brand value, and competitiveness. Uber (transport service), Alibaba (e-commerce), and Airbnb (urban housing) are growing in the market by improving the consumer chain and delivering satisfaction through active customer engagement and collective intelligence (Van Alstyne et al. 2016). Substitute products in the market affect the industry potential adversely and pose threat to the customer preferences. Bargaining power of buyers refers to the direct or indirect pressure tactics to force the industry to reduce prices or increase product features in view to optimize the customer value. Buyers gain power when they have choices and when their needs can be met by a substitute product or by the same product offered by another supplier (Rajagopal 2021). The attributes of crowd-based business modeling are exhibited in Figure 2.2.

The crowd-based business models are used to encourage open innovation with social features of business by encouraging people's participation as illustrated in Figure 2.2. Open innovations are supported by crowdsourcing to generate ideation and the possibilities of crowdfunding to generate resources for innovation. The social media and digital networks help firms in crowdsourcing the ideation process for innovation. Experience sharing and collective thinking as a process of psychodynamics help companies work with the crowd-based business model. Social learning and perceptual semantics through the crowdsourcing are used to identify PNS (problems, needs, and solutions) factors to develop customer-centric strategies. In addition, user-generated contents and wisdom-of-crowds help firms in implementing the crowd-based business models as illustrated in Figure 2.2.

The crowd-based innovation has trouble in developing competitiveness and creating value-based market segments. Such difficulties are encountered by the new ventures and existing small and medium enterprises, which are often weak in implementing the business model sophistication strategy. These firms aim at resolving their business problems at the bottom line of surviving market competition and manage to survive the market competition through tactical cost, time, and risk approaches. There are varying business models, and their design has become a key to performance of the firm. In fact, business model design is often associated with innovation and strategies for its commercialization. However, many firms successfully commercialize innovations despite collective intelligence and crowd-based business strategies. Crowd-based inclusive firms like Google succeeded in realizing full potential of its

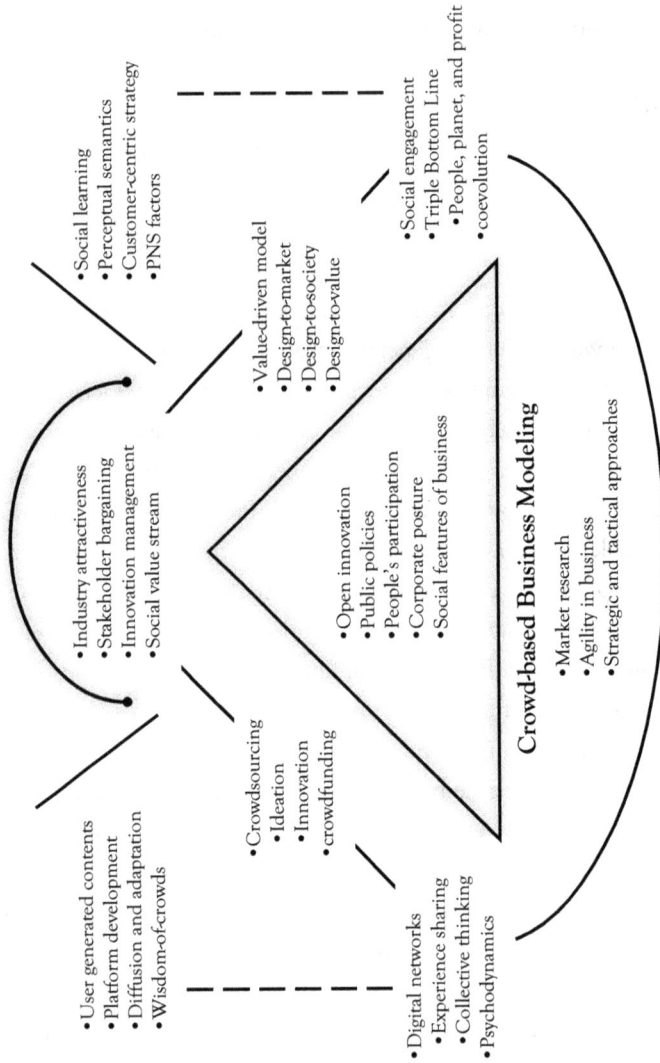

Figure 2.2 Attributes of crowd-based business modeling

Source: Author

business model by offering its main service, Internet search, completely for free and capturing value from secondary opportunities such as Google AdWords (Kesting and Günzel-Jensen 2015).

Based on various examples including Google and Ryanair, firms may derive lessons to develop a framework for business model sophistication strategies by uncovering hidden functions of innovative products and services. Firms tend to take advantage of economies of scope and scale and derive benefits to the stakeholders. The economies of scope are key economic factors that drive simultaneous manufacturing of different products with cost-effective approaches wherein the average total cost of production decreases and stimulates the production of an increasing variety of goods. Most firms adopting the crowd-based business models can utilize cross-selling opportunities and involve users, stakeholders, and the crowd in the process.

The above strategies place a strong emphasis on stakeholder commitment. The business journey of Google illustrates its way to manage crucial business model sophistication to achieve success. Google rose into the multistakeholder firm beginning its journey as a startup enterprise working with the crowd-based business model (Vise and Malseed 2005). Google has emerged as an effective and popular search engine as Internet searches created enormous benefits to consumers. However, the company could not find sustainable revenue streams to support its growth, as initially there was no willingness of users to pay for its services. As a business policy, Google had to offer its service free of charge since the beginning, which has not changed over time. Therefore, Google did not initially appear to be a promising new venture. The business strategies of Google have changed over time with the introduction of Google AdWords, a pay-per-click advertising service. The search results hold enormous value for stakeholders with a willingness to pay, and, in addition, for the firms and other players interested in being found on the Internet. However, the contemporary business model has been proved to be highly profitable (Kesting and Günzel-Jensen 2015).

Collective intelligence is also explorative, as it is able to connect firms with isolated business ideas with the success of such local experiments. The innovations developed in local markets are based on consumer needs and are marketed within niche at an affordable price to the consumers. These enterprises do not adapt to "design-to-market" innovation approach. However, the innovations with utilitarian values tend to drive high demand in local markets as they match with the socio-cultural and ethnic values. For example, in 2016, an engineer entrepreneur of India designed a low-cost clay refrigerator, which requires no electricity and keeps the cooked food fresh and safe for five days uninterruptedly. This innovative product was branded as "*mittikool*" (clay-cool). It continued to function even in the event of irregular power supplies in the rural areas. The concept of this innovation has been later adapted to the "design-to-market" strategy by a Chinese global giant Haier, which manufactured and commercialized noncompressor refrigerator. Instead of relying on a refrigerant, compressor, and evaporator to keep cool, it simply uses water and carbon dioxide (CO_2), plus a unique solid-state cooler. The product claims to save a significant amount of energy, provide more even cooling, eliminate all noise and vibration, and offer more usable space (Rajagopal 2021).

Crowdsourcing generates psychodynamics and helps in cocreating crowd-based business models aiming at doing business in consumer products in closed or open niche markets. Positive psychodynamics among consumers creates pull-effect for specific brands in the market. The pull-effect generates high consumer demand, which benefits companies in increasing market share and profit by reducing the marketing costs. Such costs for brands are spread across advertisements, in-store promotions, price discounts, and point-of-sales incentives to the consumers. The psychodynamics also generates referrals and brand advocacy behavior among consumers, which helps companies acquire new consumers at relatively low cost. Most firms involving social media as a marketing communication channel tap the knowledge and expertise of consumers for mutual benefit and for brand building process rather than adopting a traditional knowledge-management approach where people dump their information in a giant database that nobody reads. Such firms can create an environment where they go through the peer-to-peer collaboration. Emerging firms may initially build very small collaborative tools that could enable their peer communication design to kick-off the consumer-company collaboration process and to get experience in understanding how it provides mutual benefits (Rajagopal 2013).

Value-driven market environments are often obscure to the new enterprises, as it is often difficult for the firms to break the social conventions and alter consumer preferences. Such customer-based uncertainties often disrupt business models of the firms and drive them to switch to analogical thinking and reasoning (Rosenø et al. 2013). Consequently, the new market entrants often do not design value-driven business models while focusing their strategy on reducing complexity. However, focusing solely on the main business might affect the strategic growth and expansion of firms. Therefore, most firms strike a balance with identifying competitive factors and value-capturing opportunities to increase their business performance or driving new venture development (Shafer et al. 2005).

Shared Economy and Inclusivity

The shared economy has also significantly affected the business ecosystem today and the inclusivity concept in business has outgrown over time from the shared economy practices. The shared economy concept broadly refers to social innovation activities that improve the collective efficiency through crowd-based platforms and service-integration approaches such as manpower management, machines, space, services, knowledge or information, and consumable resources. Such integration is carried out by creating a pool of common resources on digital platforms in the sharing economy. The combination of sharing economy and social innovation has a great potential to deliver the corporate social responsibility (CSR), as it shares the common goal of the triple bottom line by way of involving people (inclusivity), reducing environmental impacts, focusing on the principles of reusing (sustainability), generating profit with purpose, and working closely with the business philosophy of recycling and sharing. The shared economy and inclusive business supported by the crowd behavior and collective intelligence help in cocreating and coevolving corporate social responsibility. Such business ecosystem founded on stakeholders, community leaders, public policy support, and corporate involvement drives business opportunity and community assets to align with delivering economic interests, corporate commitments, stakeholder values. The growing popularity of inclusive business models has been admired for encouraging stakeholder engagement in business planning, implementation, monitoring, and evaluation. The concept of inclusivity in business promotes liberal businesses across developing economies. However, differences exist in social governance of businesses and public policies, which affect the processes for making public policy decisions, delivering values to the stakeholders, and generating profit with purpose (Keim and Hillman 2008). Business ecosystems are more complex and work differently in the context of markets, social attributes, stakeholder culture, governance model, public policy support, and possible corporate collaboration. Complexity stems from the diversity of relationships among the key partners, key activities, and key resources, which affects the planning and implementation of business strategies in the target markets. Furthermore, many of these relationships are systemic, with companies having to influence each other indirectly. Such complexity in relationships inside the ecosystem leads to the formation of diverse structures and patterns that determine the functioning of the system within a socio-economic subdomain (Visnjic et al. 2016).

Innovations in the global marketplace have evolved from consumer needs to futuristic solutions. The evolution of markets over the centuries has been a perennial phenomenon congruent with the shifts in social, economic, and technological knowledge in the society. The evolution of business and growth has promoted economic behavior to explore the markets. Sociologically, the evolution of markets was based on the understanding that individuals are embedded in various cognitive structures involving the business activities. Shifts in the market processes in the society are induced by fundamental beliefs and shared assumptions and resemble elements of social culture defining norms of markets, expected behavior, and thought. Such business evolution paradigms are resistant to minor discrepancies between their fundamental models and contradicting (potentially empirical) evidence. Thus, discrepancies in market behavior are considered as socio-economic abnormalities, paradoxes, or puzzles in a given place and time (Rajagopal 2019).

In the growing market competition, small firms always face major threat from large firms, as the latter possess more resources (physical, finance, human resources, and technology) than the smaller firms. Hence, most of the smaller firms develop cocooning attitude and confine to a niche, as they could not continue their struggle for existence in the marketplace. It may be observed that large firms often enter into new market niches created by small firms through technological innovation and ingest the market share of small firms. In view of the Darwinian theory, it may be argued that market conditions and company-specific characteristics explain entry timing and the underlying goals of the large firms. Such entry might be a continuous process for large firms in different marketplaces. The dominating behavior of large firms is more likely to be backed by the innovations in response to the competing firms. Small firms are affected by the entry of firms that are similar in size and resources. When a highly similar company enters the new market, it raises the probability that the company enters beyond levels based solely on the attractiveness of the market. Hence, small firms play aggressively and defensively to stay in the marketplace despite the competitive attacks by new entrants. On the contrary, consortium of small firms manufacturing identical products also poses major threat to large firm in sustaining the competitive marketplace (Rajagopal 2018).

Consumer-led innovations are driven by the 4A-factors comprising awareness, availability, affordability, and adaptability reviewing the innovation life cycle, sustainability, and scope to upgrade the technology embedded in the innovations. Industry-focused innovations are largely directed toward building new markets, acquiring new clients, achieving market leadership, and reinforcing corporate image in business-to-business market environment. Most of the innovative business projects are developed around the objectives of enhancing productivity with zero defects through lean manufacturing operations. Hence, most companies are employing automation using robotics-led innovation, and improved controls and measures. Industrial innovations have random growth in the marketplace driven by the emerging "startups" across the countries that offer new insights to the companies for their business growth. Inclusive innovations have emerged out of the crowdsourcing and exploring collective intelligence to drive ideas on innovation. Social media has significantly transformed the human behavior on interpersonal communication to share ideas and experiences. With the advancement of information technology, the communication interface platforms have rapidly evolved to create a new data-driven paradigm. The crowd-based and collective communication platforms such as social media channels and micro blogs use data-intensive digital environments to communicate, collaborate, express opinions, and support decisions. Accordingly, social media and innovation have become symbiotic as the social media offer source of collective information for value cocreation by empowering individuals to actively express opinions and sentiment on all facets of interactions (Adikari et al. 2021).

In the innovation ambiance, companies and startups realize that they have to coexist and identify new ways to influence each other for managing innovative business projects and segment performance. This experience paved the way for the get-into-business stage, in which startup enterprises and large companies could manage successful businesses. In the process, startup enterprises learned business discipline from the private sector, while corporations gained innovative insights to lead the marketplace. Increased success on both sides has laid the foundation for cocreating the innovation, in which companies deliver high value to stakeholders. Alternatively, nongovernment organizations (NGOs) also actively collaborate with the companies in diffusing the innovation. When Bharat Petroleum (BP) sought to market a dual-fuel portable stove in India, it set up one such cocreation system with three Indian NGOs. The system allowed BP to bring the innovative stove to a geographically dispersed market through numerous local distributors. While the company sold its stoves profitably, the NGOs gained access to a lucrative revenue stream that could fund other innovative business projects (Prahalad and Brugmann 2007). Customer-centric companies such as LEGO, Starbucks Coffee, and Fab India believe in innovation by creating value creation that will shift the business culture from products and services to experience environments and cocreation of innovations. The experience innovations carried out in the companies not only improve the product or service but also enable the need-based cocreation of an environment in which personalized, evolvable innovation can be nurtured. The success of customer-centric innovations grows out of individual consumers cocreating their own unique value, and consumer communities on the digital platform support the companies to appropriately diffuse the innovation across the consumer segments. Over the period, consumer networks, social communication, and adaptive learning are fostering experience innovation in the multinational companies such as Sony,

Apple, Microsoft, and TiVo, illustrating the budding trend toward experience innovation (Prahalad and Ramaswamy 2003).

More business leaders are now seeking to create shared value looking at the BOP markets in response to fragmentation and disruptions in their core markets. However, the challenge in such transition is to manage systemic exploration of new opportunities and bring them into the mainstream business over time. In this context, connecting inclusive business is connected to the possibilities of innovation and venturing capabilities among firms. Most companies are attempting to stimulate inclusivity in business by empowering stakeholders in corporate social responsibility programs, which help in creating scalable social impact and connect to the core business strategy of the firm. Some of the examples of inclusive business can cite Master Card Financial Inclusion Labs, Unilever TRANSFORM program, Barclays Social Innovation Lab, Google X, and Glaxo Smith Kline Developing Market Access. These companies are making more direct investments in inclusive businesses or creating self-managed or third-party funds for ongoing "corporate impact venturing." Companies like Danone and Schneider Electric have been activity engaged with the inclusivity in business. However, most companies recognize the benefits of frugal innovation and developing low-priced innovative products, integrating them, and scaling them up to outreach Big Middle segment.

The success of new product development in most firms depends on stakeholder involvement toward ideation, interaction, identifying markets, and integration (4Is) to stimulate innovation and marketing process. The involvement of customers and investors in new product development simultaneously provides value to multiple stakeholders in supporting corporate strategies for increasing demand, stimulating buyers, and motivating users to share experiences. Such stakeholder involvement in developing and implementing corporate strategies helps firms in streamlining investments and regulators. However, firms have often observed the dilemma of downstream market stakeholder involvement which hinders customer value creation and increases performance of new products in the competitive markets. Customers with homogeneous needs are easily identifiable as stakeholder groups with active involvement in the process of innovation or new product development. However, complex markets that consist of ethnic niches exhibit heterogeneous stakeholders who play different customer roles or make a direct impact on the success of innovative products. For example, healthcare products address heterogenous stakeholders emphasizing on the needs of patients, physicians, health insurers, and regulators, each of whom has a different perception for approving, using, buying, or paying for them (Martin et al. 2021). The corporate involvement in financial, marketing, and strategic decisions is a familiar concept in conventional practices. However, the business philosophy is transforming today, with focus on inclusivity (stakeholder engagement) and optimism (social responsiveness and value creation) to stand competitive at the triple bottom line comprising people (stakeholders), planet (sustainability in business), and profit (profit-with-purpose). Firms encourage stakeholder engagement in sustainable production and use of technology in key sectors such as agriculture, energy, water conservation, and food products manufacturing.

Social Engagement and Coevolution

Social engagement is a socially responsive approach in managing tasks and socio-economic practices with expected outcomes (e.g., Henderson et al. 2012). Social engagement aligns with individual, community, civic, and institutional benefits including leverages from business and economy. While social scholarship focuses on the individual and community attributes as a state of engagement, the social perspective of engagement endorses collective impact on cocreated businesses through a socially determined process. The design-to-society philosophy is, therefore, aligned with the social engagement theory and social presence maxim, which refers to the degree of presence perceived by the community participants in generating and disseminating communication. Social presence theory argues that social media (physical and digital interactions) should align with psychological perception of involvement (presence) and transmit visual and verbal cues. Social presence broadly includes the activities of sharing ideas and experiences; communicating social postures, social brand expressions, social needs; upholding customer voice; and monitoring checks and balances on business to society value transfers (Calefato and Lanubile 2010).

The design-to-society approach is founded on the value-based business thinking, which explains the concepts of "competing with social purpose" and "performance with purpose" underlying in the welfare marketing business school of thought. The combination of design-to-society and design-to-market business philosophies connects social aspirations including the customer values to persuade market-growth needs of the companies. An effective social strategy tagged with the brand value fortifies the business goals and means. Nonetheless, it mitigates the risk of passive social associations and radical conceptualization of means to achieve performance and poses threats to stakeholder acceptance of society-linked business models. The stakeholder value can be created for all stakeholders, customers, the company, and the community at large, through strategic pursuit of brand marketing and corporate goals (Rodriguez-Vila and Bharadwaj 2017).

A social media activist may have a mix of experience with product design, marketing, software applications, and the extended reach of the communication. Companies should analyze customer experience centered on social interactions to develop community-linked marketing approaches. Such customer connectivity helps the managers stay on social media platforms like Facebook page and works with the typical customer-centric marketing tasks for a company such as working with the social media account management, and social advertising and social media campaign management. As the social networks are growing fast and gaining psychodynamics, there emerges the need for a new executive-level as the social marketing strategist, who can fully embrace the focus on social marketing. Social consciousness and business are growing simultaneously among the customers and stakeholders as a result of the ease of use of technology and transformation of communication systems from conventional wisdom to digital networks. Corporate social responsibility has become the tool to generate social consciousness and value streams to support social marketing perspectives of business. Public policies and the media have become proficient to stimulate the companies to take initiatives in developing social markets and inculcating the social consequences in the future business modeling to grow their business with the social outlooks. Consequently, the social face of business has emerged as an inescapable priority from the customer-centric companies to gain competitive leverage. Some successful business-to-customer companies like Amazon discovered Whole Foods as a social business place to generate social values and drive the business growth faster. Similarly, Toyota and Volvo have found design-to-society approaches in business more as a source of innovation and competitive advantage than a path of smooth transition of technology-oriented business in the society. Companies, while developing social imperatives in business, need to identify the social consequences of their actions and discover opportunities to benefit society and themselves by strengthening the competitive benefits. The design-to-society business modeling has, therefore, emerged as a collective thinking mindset for strategic growth of business through the social value stream (Porter and Kramer 2006).

Firms should develop social media strategies based on *Hub and Spoke model*, where a hub is located around social media. The *hub* may be led by the corporate social strategist to monitor the core communication movements within the networks and draw a framework of marketing strategy integrating customer attributes and corporate policy. The hub marketing framework needs to be further converged with the functionaries accountable in various departments of the company that denotes *spokes* in the model (Rajagopal 2021). New applications for the mobile social networking platforms are constantly appearing in the market, which have tempted many companies to tap the social network activities also from the mobile devices. A mobile device is any tool that allows access to a ubiquitous network beyond one specific access gate. The most common example of mobile device is mobile phone, but a netbook also counts if it can access different types of wireless networks such as WLAN and 3G (Kaplan 2012). Design-to-society is a community approach in developing market ecosystem on the social foundation. Most companies invest in creating social value by cocreating corporate social responsibility and developing public–private partnership by working on a social cause. Though the corporate investment in design-to-society has a long-run payback, it could play tactical in managing market competition through the social value inputs of the business. Costs and benefits of the social investment of business from the perspective of targeted growth in the marketplace often pose many challenges. Design-to-society approach to targeted community provides a significant benefit to the customers and stakeholders over the conventional for-profit marketing methods. However, in some cases, such as in sustainability projects, the social investment involves high cost in terms of either money or intangible measure (difficulty, for instance, in quitting smoking); it becomes harder for the company to connect the payback to the existing revenue streams. Social marketers face their greatest challenge in converging the intangible social benefits with business growth and performance with purpose (Rangan et al. 1996).

The business and society convergence are supported by the transformational (change in social thinking) and transactional (value-based philosophy) thinking by cocreating solutions to the societal problems related to business sector. Social marketing strategies are the effective tools to align business goals with social development and value-generation perspectives. Social innovations, sustainable development, green marketing, and implementing corporate social responsibility programs stimulate enhancement of performance with social purpose. This linear path bridging the gap between society and business validates the design-to-society and design-to-market philosophies. Social validation of marketing programs by sharing customer experiences on the digital platforms and generating user-driven contents develop the scope of cocreation of products and services effectively within the society and market. Sustainable customer products companies like IKEA, GE Energy, and Unilever focus on inducing corporate social leadership in managing the corporate social responsibility. However, while implementing society-linked business models, companies tend to develop community hubs for customer and stakeholder interactions on face-to-face, digital, or hybrid communication models. The interactions of customer on these platforms help companies document the voice-of-customers to support strategy designs. In addition, public policies, public private partnerships, and social psychodynamics leverage companies in designing programs to evolve in vulnerable social sectors (health, education, housing, agriculture, and nonfarm economic production, with meticulous business strategies (Rajagopal 2021)).

Social business is a value-led function involving customers, stakeholders, and entrepreneurs. The initiatives of involving the social entities in cocreating products and services help companies in driving quickly to social business due to wider acceptability among customers. Social businesses are more effective in reaching out to the BOP customer segment and transforming demand for innovative products. Therefore, building the social base for innovative products ensures reaping of higher gains as compared to the market-oriented competitive strategies. Cocreation is an upcoming phenomenon in business ecosystem, which involves society and business in sharing and adapting experiences of people, respectively. It is a bidirectional dynamic of exchanging ideas, experiences, innovation concepts, developing prototypes, and commercializing generic thought into the business avenues. Experience cocreation is an art, which is portrayed by the business communities with the support of personal and digital interfaces to know the insights of all players in market operations including customers. Cocreating business models with the underlying customer and stakeholder experiences have emerged as a new paradigm of strategy innovation. Customer-centric companies like Nestlé, Conagra, Amazon, Unilever, and Tata India can explore the public domain holistically today to innovate products and services with compelling value propositions through cocreating strategy with effective employee engagement (e.g. Ramaswamy and Gouillart 2008).

Case Studies

Energy Cooperatives in the Netherlands

Production and consumption of community energy is a key action toward sustainability and managing climate crisis. Empowering people through cooperative institutions helps in boosting the local economies and reinvigorate conscious consumption, sustainability, and build stakeholder values. Community-led initiatives significantly contribute to the transition of energy production through the renewable sources. Europe has many success stories of community energy projects, and the Netherlands is home to 623 energy cooperatives. However, the growth of energy cooperatives in the country has slowed down during the pandemic of COVID-19 but the capacity of generating renewable energy is continuing among the cooperatives. Likewise, all alternative energy resources and services from solar to wind, renovation, mobility, and heating have grown significantly over the years. The recent development in the local energy institutions witnessed a substantial growth of local, cooperative energy provision, fueled by public and political ambitions toward energy transition. Such grassroots energy cooperatives provision now presents a stakeholder engaged route to energy production, distribution, and consumption alongside conventional, centralized provision. However, worldwide, scaling of cooperative activities poses a challenge. The cooperatives in the Netherlands meet this challenge by forging alliances with mainstream energy companies as they have established 162 new alliances in 2016. Employing a mixed institutionalist perspective, the social and economic drivers have increased the number of alliances and reinforced the social energy value chain (de Bakker et al. 2020). The renewable energy generation through cooperative in the Netherlands has increased during 2020 as detailed below[2]:

- Collective solar power capacity grew 41 percent in 2020 as compared to 2019 with 211 projects scheduled power generation. The Netherlands count a total of 814 collective solar projects with the capacity to generate power though cooperatives to the electricity demand of almost 50,000 households.
- Cooperative wind power capacity has reached a total of 229.9 MW with an increase of 37.1 MW in 2020 as compared to 2019.

REScoops in the Netherlands are energy cooperatives, which are grown as the business model engaging citizens in the generation of renewable energy through active participation in the energy efficiency projects. These societies have a citizen charter emphasizing on collective generation and distribution of renewable energy through communities. REScoops do not necessarily have the legal statute of a cooperative, but they distinguish themselves by the way they do business. Similarly, many people and companies live and work with the sustainable power of SHREC stakeholder Energie VanOns,[3] an energy collective in the Netherlands. The sustainable power is generated through many big and

---

[2] For details see Rescoops Newsletter, www.rescoop.eu/news-and-events/news/february-success-story-the-rising-tide-of-dutch-cooperatives (Retrieved on March 06, 2022).

[3] For details see SHREC Interreg Europe website, www.interregeurope.eu/shrec/news/news-article/8327/energy-cooperatives-united-in-the-netherlands/ (Retrieved on March 06, 2022).

small projects and delivers about 25.7 million KW energy to the community. Business and governments also support the locally generated green energy. The organization aims to unite 1,000 cooperatives with 5,000 projects to generate power and to reach 1,00,000 customers.

With the increasing systemic transformation in the energy system, there is a consistent decline in the prices of renewable energy. Simultaneously, the conscious participation of people in energy cooperatives and increasing policy commitments, investments, and engagement of incumbent business has made the renewable energy sector growth-oriented. However, there is a long way to go for the cooperative energy movement to develop strategic capacity to generate and distribute energy by matching the increasing demand. The ability to mobilize people toward a common vision through encouragement needs a transformational leadership (Weathersby 1999). These cooperatives have emerged as a peer-to-peer energy market mechanism, which regulates the peers' trading behaviors and does business by the market-clearing process. These social institutions match energy demand with supply and settle the time, price, and volume of the trades. The cost-sharing mechanism shares the cost and benefits among the stakeholders (Liu et al. 2017).

Probiotech Agribusiness in Nepal

Agriculture is the primary economic sector of Nepal, which contributes over one-third of share to the gross domestic product of the country. The marginal and small farmers of the country typically cultivate less than one acre of land and find it difficult to expand their farms and increase their incomes due to the lack of training, inputs, and finance. Probiotech, a leading processor and producer of animal health and nutrition products in Nepal, has significantly contributed to the success of small farmers. The company is engaged with the farmers at both ends of its product deliveries and value chain. Probiotech focuses on farming communities and uses institutional funding to finance manufacturing capacity for value-added products like soy flour, nuggets, and refined oil. Such resource channelization helps the company to increase sourcing from over 8,000 farmers and food suppliers and improve food safety standards. Probiotech is a subsidiary of agribusiness-focused business house, NIMBUS Holdings. Nepal, in partnership with International Finance

Corporation, has invested $3.8 million in feed manufacturer Probiotech Industries to enhance poultry farm productivity and boost incomes in rural Nepal. This investment emerged to strengthen the poultry supply chain in Nepal through training the female farmers.

The principal input in developing cattle and poultry feed is maize, and the company sources it for its animal feed products from grain farmers. The company offers best cultivation practices to the farmers engaged in growing inputs required for the feed manufacturing plant. Probiotech also engages small enterprises to distribute its animal feed products to poultry and livestock producers, with poultry farms accounting for 90 percent of the company's total feed sales. Many poultry customers run small-scale operations under the high production costs and other inefficiencies. The company has adopted inclusive business model which engages stakeholders (farmers and customers) in both manufacturing and marketing processes of cattle and poultry feed. By building capacity and facilitating access to input finance across its value chain, Probiotech has brought tangible economic benefits to the small farmers in Nepal.

Initially, the company faced several challenges including low-quality inputs, limited market linkages, limited access to finance, and insufficient technical knowledge among the stakeholders. Such problems have deterred the company from adopting the inclusive business practices. Addressing these issues strategically has provided an opportunity for the company to build loyalty among farmers and help them grow their coordinated operations. The agribusiness ecosystem in Nepal indicated that poultry required a large quantity of feed to obtain sufficient nutrition to produce meat or eggs. However, farmers using the conventional feed could not achieve optimal returns. Since many poultry producers in Nepal are women, the inclusive business model of the company has significantly increased their participation. Childcare was provided at trainings, which were scheduled at convenient times, since family responsibilities often prevented women from attending events. In addition, female veterinarians were trained to provide extension support. Probiotech established a farm extension unit and later embedded it within the company. Probiotech also leveraged helplines, veterinarians, and distributors to further engage and support poultry producers. The inclusive business model of the company has helped small-scale producers across rural Nepal by engaging them holistically in the agribusiness process.

References

Adikari, A., D. Burnett, D. Sedera, D. de Silva, and D. Alahakoon. 2021. "Value Co-Creation for Open Innovation: An Evidence-Based Study of the Data Driven Paradigm of Social Media Using Machine Learning." *International Journal of Information Management Data Insights* 1, no. 2. (in press). https://doi.org/10.1016/j.jjimei.2021.100022

Bughin, J. December 2014. *Three-Ways Companies Can Make Co-Creation Pay-Off.* McKinsey Insight. New York, NY: McKinsey & Co.

Calefato, F., and F. Lanubile. 2010. "Communication Media Selection for Remote Interaction of *ad hoc* Groups." In *Advances in Computers* 78, pp. 271–313. Elsevier.

Chamberlain, W., and W. Anseeuw. 2019. "Inclusiveness Revisited: Assessing Inclusive Businesses in South African Agriculture." *Development Southern Africa* 36, no. 5, pp. 600–615.

de Bakker, M., A. Lagendijk, and M. Wiering. 2020. "Cooperatives, Incumbency, or Market Hybridity: New Alliances in the Dutch Energy Provision." *Energy Research & Social Science* 61 (in press). https://doi.org/10.1016/j.erss.2019.101345

Desai, H.P. 2014. "Business Models for Inclusiveness." *Procedia—Social and Behavioral Sciences* 157, pp. 353–362.

Fedorenko, I., P. Berthon, and T. Rabinovich. 2017. "Crowded Identity: Managing Crowdsourcing Initiatives to Maximize Value for Participants Through Identity Creation." *Business Horizons* 60, no. 2, pp. 155–165.

German, L.A., A.M. Bonanno, L.C. Foster, and L. Cotula. 2020. "'Inclusive Business' in Agriculture: Evidence From the Evolution of Agricultural Value Chains." *World Development* 134, (in Press). https://doi.org/10.1016/j.worlddev.2020.105018

Hart, S., S. Sharma, and M. Halme. 2016. "Poverty, Business Strategy, and Sustainable Development." *Organization & Environment* 29, no. 4, pp. 401–415.

Henderson, A., S.D. brown, and S.M. Pancer. 2012. "Political and Social Dimensions of Civic Engagement: The Impact of Compulsory Community Service." *Politics & Policy* 40, pp. 93–130.

Ji, Y., and S. Kim. 2019. "Crisis-Induced Public Demand for Regulatory Intervention in the Social Media Era: Examining the Moderating Roles of Perceived Government Controllability and Consumer Collective Efficacy." *New Media & Society* 22, no. 6, pp. 959–983.

Kaplan, A.M. 2012. "If You Love Something, Let It Go Mobile: Mobile Marketing and Mobile Social Media 4x4." *Business Horizons* 55, no. 2, pp. 129–139.

Keim, G.D., and A.J. Hillman. 2008. "Political Environments and Business Strategy: Implications for Managers." *Business Horizons* 51, no. 1, pp. 47–53.

Kesting, P., and F. Günzel-Jensen. 2015. "SMEs and New Ventures Need Business Model Sophistication." *Business Horizons* 50, no. 3, pp. 285–293.

Kietzmann, J.H. 2017. "Crowdsourcing: A Revised Definition and an Introduction to New Research." *Business Horizons* 60, no. 2, pp. 151–153.

Kohler, T. 2015. "Crowdsourcing-Based Business Models: How to Create and Capture Value." *California Management Review* 57, no. 4, pp. 63–84.

Liu N., X. Yu, C. Wang, C. Li, L. Ma, and J. Lei. 2017. "Energy-Sharing Model With Price-Based Demand Response for Microgrids of Peer-to-Peer Prosumers." *IEEE Transactions on Power Systems* 32, no. 5, pp. 3569–3583.

Livingston, B.A., and T.R. Opie. 2019. *Even at "Inclusive" Companies, Women of Color Don't Feel Supported.* Harvard Business Review Digital Article, Cambridge, MA: Harvard Business School Press.

Malone, T.W., R.J. Laubacher, and C. Dellarocas. 2010. "The Collective Intelligence Genome." *MIT Sloan Management Review* 51, no. 3, pp. 21–31.

Martin, P., L. Lizarondo, S. Kumar, and D. Snowdon. 2021. "Impact of Clinical Supervision on Healthcare Organisational Outcomes: A Mixed Methods Systematic Review." *PLoS One* 16, no. 11, p. e0260156. (in press). https://doi.org/10.1371/journal.pone.0260156.

McFalls, R. 2017. *Good Procurement Practices and SMEs in Supply Chains: Nespresso AAA Sustainable Quality Program Impact of Procurement Practices in an SME in Colombia.* Geneva: International Labor Organization.

Mont, O., Y.V. Palgan, K. Bradley, and L. Zvolska. 2020. "A Decade of the Sharing Economy: Concepts, Users, Business and Governance Perspectives." *Journal of Cleaner Production* 269 (in Press). https://doi.org/10.1016/j.jclepro.2020.122215

Porter, M.E., and M.R. Kramer. 2006. "Strategy and Society: The Link Between Competitive Advantage and Corporate Social Responsibility." *Harvard Business Review* 84, no. 12, pp. 78–92.

Prahalad, C.K., and A. Hammond. 2002. "Serving the World's Poor, Profitably." *Harvard Business Review* 80, no. 9, pp. 48–57.

Prahalad, C.K., and J. Brugmann. 2007. "Cocreating Business's New Social Compact." *Harvard Business Review* 85, no. 2, pp. 80–90.

Prahalad, C.K., and V. Ramaswamy. 2003. "New Frontier of Experience Innovation." *MIT Sloan Management Review* 44, no. 4, pp. 12–18.

Rajagopal. 2013. *Managing Social Media and Consumerism: The Grapevine Effect in Competitive Markets.* Basingstoke, UK: Palgrave Macmillan.

Rajagopal. 2018. *Consumer Behavior Theories: Convergence of Divergent Perspectives With Applications to Marketing and Management.* New York, NY: Business Expert Press.

Rajagopal. 2019. *Contemporary Marketing Strategy: Analyzing Consumer Behavior to Drive Managerial Decision Making.* New York, NY: Palgrave Macmillan.

Rajagopal. 2021. *The Business Design Cube: Converging Markets, Society, and Customer Values to Grow Competitive in Business.* New York, NY: Business Expert Press.

Ramaswamy, V., and F.J. Gouillart. 2008. *Co-Creating Strategy With Experience Co-Creation.* Harvard Business School Newsletter, Cambridge: Harvard Business School Press.

Rangan, V.K., S. Karim, and S.K. Sandberg. 1996. "Do Better at Doing Good." *Harvard Business Review* 74, no. 3, pp. 42–54.

Ritzer, G. 2014. "Prosumption: Evolution, Revolution, or Eternal Return of the Same?" *Journal of Consumer Culture* 14, no. 1, pp. 3–24.

Rodriguez-Vila, O., and S. Bharadwaj. September–October 2017. "Competing on Social Purpose." *Harvard Business Review*, pp. 94–101.

Rosenø, A., E. Enkel, and F. Mezger. 2013. "Distinctive Dynamic Capabilities for New Business Creation: Sensing, Seizing, Scaling and Separating." *International Journal of Technology Marketing* 8, no. 2, pp. 197–234.

Sawmy, M.V. 2015. "Growing Inclusive Business Models in the Extractive Industries: Demonstrating a Smart Concept to Scale Up Positive Social Impacts." *The Extractive Industries and Society* 2, no. 4, pp. 676–679.

Scheyvens, R., G. Banks, and E. Hughes. 2016. "The Private Sector and the SDGs: The Need to Move Beyond 'Business as Usual'." *Sustainable Development* 24, no. 6, pp. 371–382.

Shafer, S.M., H.J. Smith, and J. Lindner. 2005. "The Power of Business Models." *Business Horizons* 48, no. 3, pp. 199–207.

Shainesh, G., and S. Kulkarni. 2016. *Aravind Eye Care's Vision Centers-Reaching Out to the Rural Poor.* Cambridge, MA: Harvard Business School Press.

Shi, H. 2021. "The Application of Social Psychology and Collective Internet Governance," *Aggression and Violent Behavior.* (*in Press*). https://doi .org/10.1016/j.avb.2021.101588

Stainer, A., and L. Stainer. 1998. "Business Performance: A Stakeholder Approach." *International Journal of Business Performance and Management* 1, no. 1, pp. 2–12.

Van Alstyne, M.W., G. Parker, and S.P. Choudary. 2016. "Pipelines, Platforms, and the New Rules of Strategy." *Harvard Business Review* 94, no. 4, pp. 54–62.

Vise, D.A., and M. Malseed. 2005. *The Google Story.* New York, NY: Delacorte Press.

Visnjic, I., A. Neely, C. Cennamo, and N. Visnjic. 2016. "Governing the City: Unleashing Value From the Business Ecosystem." *California Management Review* 59, no. 1, pp. 109–140.

Weathersby, G.B. 1999. "Leadership vs. Management." *Management Review* 88, no. 3, p. 5.

Yamkovenko, B., and S. Tavares. 2017. *To Understand Whether Your Company Is Inclusive, Map How Your Employees Interact.* Harvard Business Review Digital Article. Cambridge, MA: Harvard Business School Press.

CHAPTER 3

Collective Business Decisions

Continuous learning is the vital process in social- and customer-centric businesses (Schön 2017). It emphasizes as how lessons can be drawn from the success and failure experiences in doing business with people. The pace at which organizations learn may become the only sustainable source of competitive advantage over time (Senge 19990). The participatory business appraisal as a new concept has been discussed as a continuous learning tool by engaging customers, stakeholders, and crowd within the business ecosystem. Participatory appraisals are used as a driver to actions research in resolving social issues and analyzing the cultural, biological, and legal perspectives to promote customer-centric businesses on a social scale (Chambers 1994). This chapter discusses the attributes of community workplace, experience sharing, and collective intelligence. In addition, the discussion on inclusive marketing-mix and corporate social responsibility also leads the chapter. There are three case studies discussed in this chapter comprising ITC Agribusiness (India), Shakti experiment of Hindustan Unilever Limited (India), and Sodexo, a French food services and facilities companies.

Community Workplace

The workplace learning motivates employee engagement and is driven by a wider community which encourages transformation in the work process and continuous learning in the organization. Learning is viewed as a continuous organizational process that enables the firm to achieve distinctions in the various organizational processes. Working and learning activities grow together in competitive enterprises to deal with complex issues. Community learning identifies learning as a part of social practice which takes place within the community ecosystem of practice through participatory training process. Learning in community workplaces is managed by knowledge sharing through the participatory skill-development programs by encouraging experience sharing, developing concept maps, and goal-oriented project planning approaches. The employee and stakeholder participation in knowledge management (creation and diffusion) plays an important role in developing community workplace as an effective center of practice in an organization. The emerging workplace model for inclusive business organizations is through building work-related portfolios and developing participatory practices with clear accountability. The workplace environment in inclusive businesses is linked with collective competency framework and identifying organizational development needs. The community workplaces can be facilitated by a mentor for specific work portfolios and encouraging employees and stakeholders to undertake activities collectively or by constituting specialty teams. This process facilitates workplace-based learning tools that increase the capabilities and competencies of employees and provide formative feedback and opportunities to discuss experiences with peers. Ideally, the work portfolios in an organization demonstrate learned and best practice, employee achievements, continuous learning, and developing plans for future. An inclusive workplace starts at the top of the organization and is followed across the work portfolios throughout the company. Managers have the responsibility to foster the inclusivity in corporate culture. Employee teams need to be trained in collective work culture and inclusive behavior to stay along the diversity and inclusion initiatives of the companies. It is necessary for a healthy organization to create a workplace where every employee accepts the inclusive business culture.

Competency concept maps by work portfolios can be developed by the organization with the community workplace. The knowledge management frameworks enable employees and stakeholders of the organization to identify the development needs of the firm in the context of the community and target market. Accordingly, training, participation, and learning structures are developed by the firms operating with the inclusive business models. However, as individuals may lack self-assessment skills to identify appropriate development areas, the community workplace design is developed by the firms to enhance the contemporary knowledge and skills of employees and stakeholders. The degree of learning opportunities in the workplace varies by corporate workplace policies, projects, and future alliances with the other organizations. The corporate trainer engaged in imparting knowledge and skills to the employees and stakeholders is both education supervisor and mentor. Workplace trainers also provide support to employees and stakeholders by identifying personal development needs and business requirements. Inclusive organizational practices in the social contexts help in developing workplace relationship among peers. In inclusive workplaces, the formation of work relationships among co-workers grows as resources for personal achievements and emerges as relationship channels through which employees might identify workplace solidarity and engage in collective action. The workplace ecosystem has several psychosocial factors such as common goals, emotions, and leadership that influence the workplace culture, practices, and ecosystems. Workplace relationships provide access to resources and social networks at work, which affect a wide range of organizational and individual benefits at work. Informal networks develop trust among the co-workers within firm and affect organizational productivity. A structure of a social system of an organization has four principal factors comprising leadership, employees, goals, and stakeholders that affect the workplace culture, creativity, and innovation. Additionally, workplace relationships depend on clarity of communications, transparency in policies, creative commons, and opportunities to work on innovative projects with the peers. Relationships in the inclusive workplace environment attribute good intentions among peers and help continue interacting with each in a positive context and practice collectivistic management approach (Shore et al. 2018).

Community workplace has been observed as a joyful workplace to deal with the social cognition, entrepreneurial stress, business fatigue, and burn-out in innovating new products. The shared peer-to-peer workplace within social enterprises provides proactive approach that inculcates the sense of belongingness, appreciation, well-being in the members of the team, and working together for predetermined entrepreneurial goals. The sense of community toward pursuing common entrepreneurial goals requires a commitment to the mission, vision, and values of the enterprise. These tenets are often created to drive organic consensus in stakeholder and put them in action by a team with transformational leadership. Inclusive business organizations conduct periodical assessments to ensure stakeholder loyalty and commitment and inculcate positive attitude. Stakeholder engagement can be encouraged by creation of psychosocial workplace, which could offer mindfulness, and stress-free lifestyle choices. Such workplace environment would develop sensitivity toward the task management and organization and motivate collaboration between the stakeholders and employees (Jalilianhasanpour et al. 2021). The product improvement and business modeling can be developed by enhancing the backgrounds and experiences of the employees, stakeholders, and the organization. Diverse perspectives of community workplace are essential to promote innovation and creativity. The inclusivity in business and community workplace is integrated in a Hummii, a chickpea ice cream startup of United States.

Hummii Snacks is a consumer product brand which has a short product-mix supported by the Hummii Meta Media, which includes Web 3.0 focused on fitness, food, and entertainment within the community. The company encourages diverse team backgrounds by drawing on their cultural diversity to inspire new flavors and product promotions. The community workplace helps the organization to analyze the voice of employees and develop creative initiatives to stay competitive in the marketplace. Collective working in a community workplace can set up interpersonal space for discussions and collaborate with the management to elicit constructive feedback on diverse issues. Inclusive businesses largely depend on the community workstations and tend to institutionalize collective work culture. Though employees in community workplace commonly constitute preferred groups, a common goal and approach do not restrict them toward creativity and collective decision making. Such community workplace engagements integrate varied perceptions across social segments of employees and stakeholders. However, some social disadvantages prevail in the workplace in every major economy around the world (Ingram 2021). The attributes of community workplace and engagement of stakeholders and customers have been exhibited in Figure 3.1.

The community workplace in organizations provides space to employees and stakeholders for thinking, creativity, decision making, and

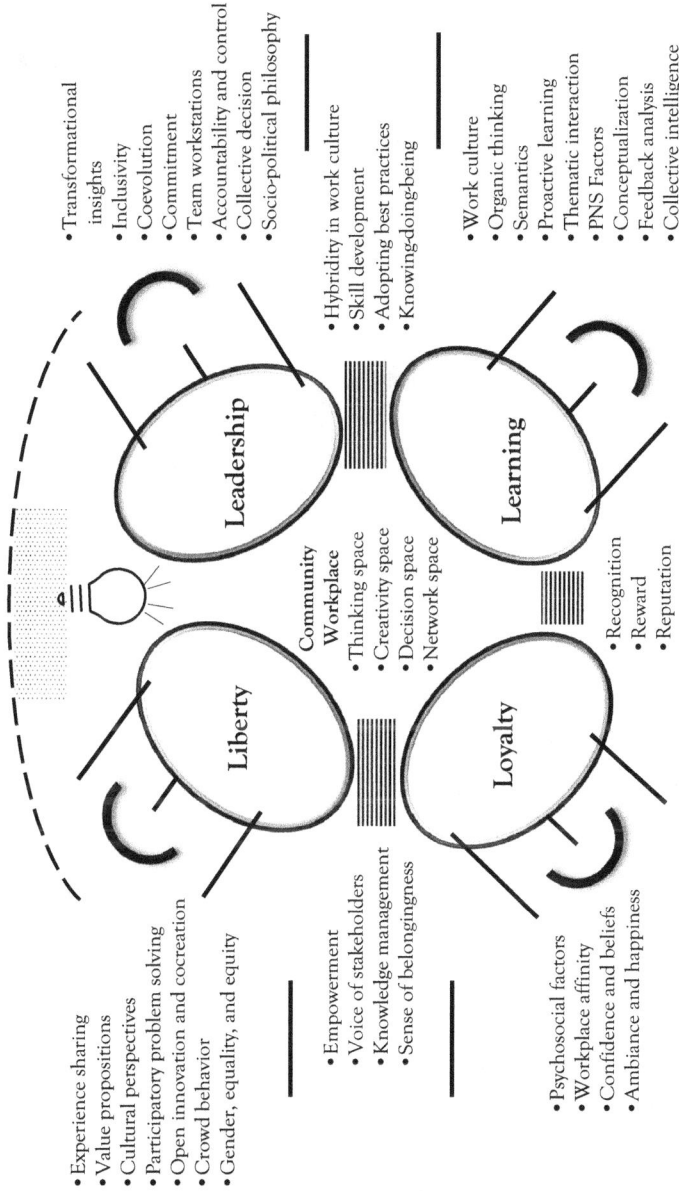

Figure 3.1 Community workplace, ambience, and engagements

Source: Author

developing relationship among the peers, stakeholders, and customers as illustrated in Figure 3.1. The community workplace also supports employees and stakeholders in an organization with the 4L factors comprising leadership, learning, loyalty, and liberty. The transformational leadership insights in growing organizations encourage inclusivity at workplace coevolve with the reverse accountability and control. The transformational leadership motivates collective actions on decisions at team workstations with commitment to stay innovative and competitive in the marketplace. Effective leadership also motivates continuous learning for employees and tunes the work culture of the organization with contemporary requirements. The community workplace provides the scope of organic thinking among the employees and stakeholders, which helps in developing inclusivity in business. Organic thinking is like brainstorming, which emerges out of interaction with peers and proactive debates in the community workplace. Organic thoughts are born out of thematic interactions within the society, organization, and teams, when inflow of thoughts is supported by the mental space and freedom of expression. The organic thinking helps companies discover, define, and develop semantics, and deliver the concepts and applications on the PNS related to the stakeholders, customers, and society at large. The proactive learning, thematic interactions, and collective intelligence help community workplaces to serve as vital organizational source for ideation, thought processing, innovation, commercialization, and profit-making.

Loyalty in the community workplace is driven by various psychosocial factors such as self-esteem and developing social concepts as exhibited in Figure 3.1. The workplace affinity, confidence among employees, social and personal beliefs, and ambience of the workplace create loyalty among the employees and stakeholders. Loyalty in the community workplace is reinforced by freedom at work, empowerment, and knowledge management. Such workplace culture inculcates the sense of belongingness among employees and stakeholders. Agility in organization offers flexibility in learning, analyzing problems, and decision making among employees through experience sharing. In addition, the liberal workplace environment motivates open innovation and cocreation. The leadership in agile organizations develops hybrid work culture (a combination of online and offline work system), offers skill development embedding continuous learning to adapt to the best practices of industry, and encapsulates the holistic organizational philosophy of knowing (learning), doing (practicing), and being (self-actualization).

The community workplace, organizational ambience, and employee engagements deteriorate with the decline in performance of the firms, which leads to fail over time. The loyalty of employees is significantly affected in the organization as these firms tend to fail. Firms must develop a viability systems approach with effective leadership during the turbulent situations (Elezi et al. 2013). The leadership and management of an organization need to be planned to stand out the turbulent environment in firms, which demands intricated planning for the future (Knowles and Saxberg 1988). Bureaucratic systems might not support such eventualities of firms today but collective preparedness to manage these unanticipated events, crises, and unthinkable requires effective employee coordination and commitment. The top management must ensure flexibility and fluidity in the organization by improving the ability of employees to function in organic and open-system relationships (Scaliza et al. 2022).

Socio-political approaches applied to the governance of urban transport and logistics services encourage human involvement to maximum limits and avoid mechanical interventions for improving sustainability. Services behavior, transport demand, cargo dynamics, and investment decisions are often explained by aggregating the supply-chain behavior. The social and cultural resources interpret and analyze the dynamics involved in a systemwide transformation initiative to attain sustainability. Mumbai-based *Dabbawala*[1] organization achieves high service performance at par with the lean management and six-sigma paradigm with a cost-effective simple operating system. The delivery system embodies mission, information management, material flows, human resource system, operations processes to meet the growing requirements, and challenges

---

[1] In Mumbai, one of the largest cosmopolitan cities in South-east Asia, *Dabbawala* (lunch-box delivery person) is a conventional logistics and transportation system for delivering the food packs to the thousands of employees working in various organizations within the city. *Dabbawala* organization use bicycles, motorcycles, delivery vans, and public transport to deliver food packs.

of home-cooked food delivery. It is a sustainable way of delivery system. As the city grew, the demand for Dabba delivery grew too. The conventional coding system is still prominent in the 21st century. Initially it was a simple color coding but now since Mumbai is a widely spread metro with three local train routes, coding has also evolved into alphanumeric characters. An outside consultant proposed the introduction of new technologies and management systems, while the leading logistics companies (e.g., FedEx) come to Mumbai to learn about the *Dabbawala* system (Thomke and Sinha 2010). Digital *Dabbawala* is an initiative to combine technology, e-initiatives of the state government. This organization has six-sigma certification (Forbes Magazine) that engages over 5,000 human resources working in Mumbai to deliver over 200,000 lunch boxes each day. The e-deliveries are managed by registering clients in the organizational system, which enables a delivery person (*Dabbawala*) to come with a laptop and a biometric device and register client's agreement through the validation of social security card. The service begins after the registration is successful. This logistics and transportation organization has been ISO 9001:2000 certified by the Joint Accreditation System of Australia and New Zealand.

The value proposition of both customers and social communities contributes significantly in the sustainable business modeling process. Value proposition describes the attributes of product/service offering, the customer segments, and their relationship in the social deliveries, while value creation and delivery describe how value is provided to customers (the channel efficiency and value delivery process) including the structure and activities in the value chain (Osterwalder and Pigneur 2010). There are various layers of business value creation in crowd-funded businesses. At the bottom-of-the-pyramid (BOP), the value chain model includes mainly informational-, emotional-, esteem-, and commitment factors, which positively influence the value creation process. The intermediate level of social value creation is developed by establishing relationships with stake holders that enables sharing of information, cocreation, and coevolution process of social innovation and business projects. The apex level of social value creation has been identified as the sense of belongingness among the stakeholders of sustainable business projects. In addition, collaborative projects promoting stakeholder engagements in managing sustainable projects, innovations, and technologies contribute to the social value creation (Liu et al. 2020). The value-chain management and deliveries of sustainable business projects show effective results when organizations follow collaborative work culture with autonomy and employee engagement. The corporate social responsibility projects of most multinational companies are implemented as a pilot to test the sustainability-based business model. Such business philosophy emphasizes stakeholder and customer needs, and defines ways through which companies deliver value to them, invest in value creation, and cocreate resources through the proper design and operation of the various elements of the value chain (Tecee 2010).

Collective Decisions

Leadership plays a crucial role in business governance and influences the best practices that are cocreated and coevolved within the organization. However, the governance patterns differ with the public- (state), crowd- (community), and private-funded business firms. The best practices in business governance irrespective of size of the firm are largely affected by a collaged system of organizational culture, social conventions, regulations, and a mix of public and private policies. Such governance system in small and medium companies functions with no accepted metric for determining the key performance indicators leading to measure success. Crowd-based businesses have collective leadership involving stakeholders and externally chosen business leader (as Chief Executive Officer), which serves as core decision-making unit. The collective governance is a social redesign built on the following maxims (Subramanian 2015):

- The governing board is constituted by the stakeholder comprising customers and investors.
- Board exercises the right to manage the company for the long term.
- Business leaders collectively make decisions on business operations and systematically guide performance with purpose.
- Streamlining corporate earnings and inclusive growth provisions.

- Boards should explore and induct an organizational to select best possible people in the boardroom. This requires effective performance evaluations of directors and a consideration of shareholder proxy access.
- Boards should give shareholders an orderly voice. Instead of defending the corporate policies, develop a reasonable process for shareholders to make decision on various issues.

One of the major challenges in managing stakeholder values in crowd-based businesses is to define long-term objectives and risk factors and encourage stakeholders to invest with predetermined value propositions. Major investors in crowd-based business models focused on sustainability, consumer well-being, and social innovations; commercial frugal innovations set a multiyear time frame for payback and creating value. Accordingly, stakeholders decide how much underperformance they can tolerate in the short term in specific markets (niche or competitive markets) to align their investments with this business agenda of the firm. Effective stakeholder engagement drives an active sense of ownership or belongingness of the firm. Big investors cultivate ongoing relationships with the companies over time as they plan to invest more in diversified business projects and tend to collaborate with management to optimize corporate strategy and governance. Often, investors demand strategic metrics from firms to improve their investment decision and value propositions. A collective structure institutional governance in the crowd-based business projects usually supports short-term approach. However, potential social and commercial intertwined business projects develop strategic vision and performance metrics to provide a precise growth-linked dashboard to the investors. Big investors gain confidence with competent board members who are committed to ensure long-term performance in business as well as extend support in developing collaborative policies and governance to philosophy into action (Barton and Wiseman 2014).

The open system business governance is common in crowd-based businesses, which encourage proportional representation of customers, stakeholders, long-term investors, and crowd leaders in the collective governance process through a formal board setup. As most crowd-funded projects are initiated in the social businesses or social innovation projects, the social leaders who are engaged in the noncommercial (social value creation), transformational (driving social tasks from conventional wisdom to digital and automated technologies), and inspirational (spiritual and art of life) leadership practices contribute to the social businesses. Crowd-funded social businesses are encouraged to have total or partial community governance backed by the nongovernmental organizations or progressive youth leaders. Both the open and social business governance systems are influenced by the social value system. In these forms of business governance, social benefits of the business have higher priority as compared to revenue generation and profitability. The corporate governance system of crowd-funded business firms tends to follow bottom-up governance model by accommodating the customers, investors, and employees in managing the firm. In the bottom-up governance system, corporate decisions are initiated, processed, and endorsed by the governing body comprising the stakeholders, customers, alliance partners, and employees. Grameen Bank model of Bangladesh, dairy farmers cooperatives in Japan and India, and microfinance institutions in Mexico are good examples of the bottom-up governance. However, the boards of public enterprises, which constitute public equities and government capital resources, are headed by the social and political representatives or civil servants. The recent shift in the business philosophy has influenced companies operating in public and private resources to develop business model to integrate the design-to-market, design-to-society, and design-to-value-based governance system. However, there also exists mixed-governance system in many regional and international companies which combine the representation of stakeholders, customers, employees, society, and government entities in the formal board structure (Rajagopal 2021).

Hybrid governance model is an emerging phenomenon in the corporate world. In this model, a large number of representations from various groups (stakeholders, customers, technology experts, government, financial institutions, and social platforms) occupy the middle ground in the state-owned, public-sector enterprises, and fully privatized companies operating in emerging markets. Sizable government stakes in leading industries in the form of ownership, management, subsidies, or other forms of preferential treatment are found common in the companies.

Such shifts are both market-driven and regulatory, which lead to hybrid governance with a blend of human resources, technology, and regulatory framework. The hybrid governance helps firms in multistakeholder management, crowd-funded business projects, and publicly financed corporations that compete in the local and global marketplaces (Khanna 2012). The hybrid governance also encourages public–private partnership in businesses and induces crowd cognition and collective controls (commons), which operate with strategic goals and operational plans.

Nonetheless, corporate governance is not all about investment, power, and profit. Governance is about ensuring that decisions are made effectively that contribute to business performance, create develop new alliances, and create corporate value. Good governance helps in building power relationships with stakeholders, key business players, employees, and customers. A good bottom-up governance (crowd-based, social, and customer-led governance) needs a system in which senior managers and the company's board collaborate on decision making and regularly seek the input of shareholders to develop and implement cocreated and coevolved strategies. The key requirements in improving the governance system of a firm are to drive the collective role of directors and induce positive contributions of key players in business. They must have expertise on the corporate finance, administration, and technology management. The board, stakeholders, key collaborators, and customers should be aware of business procedures and be able to focus on new strategies through brainstorming on the business needs under the current market ecosystem. Only reviewing past performance will not be adequate to establish good business governance. In order to achieve effective governance outcomes in the firm, directors need better access to company information so that they can devote substantial time to the corporation and their compensation should be linked to equity performance. In addition, managers, board members, and shareholders must set up lines of regular and direct communication (Pound 1995).

The social governance in crowd-based businesses is more effective than the conventional top-down governance model. Firms experience better performance through collective or coevolved business governance model by inducting customers and crowd-led investors in decision making and building competitive strategies of the firm. Crowd-based firms aim at motivating behavioral change through collective leadership designed in a democratic pattern with design-to-society and design-to-value business philosophies. However, it is often difficult for firms to sustain the market competition due to the lack of streamlined leadership and a predetermined business philosophy. The major challenge with the crowd-based firms is ensuring performance and competitiveness for the long run. Often firms growing with crowd-funding tend to develop alliance with social networks and engage in media advocacy to complement to a social marketing program. Commonly, the crowd-based businesses operated through the social marketing programs are intervened by the social conventions, local politics, and community organizations to gain social support. For example, a healthcare company may involve social networks to disseminate knowledge about the breast cancer, and diagnosis and treatments associated with it. Though this issue might be raised by the healthcare company as a social marketing debate, but it also appears to be an issue to be addressed by the local nongovernmental organizations and the local politics. Hence this product of crowd-funded social health clinics in a social network could attract any of these behaviors getting an annual mammogram as a mix of social-commercial issue, seeing a physician each year for a breast exam as a matter of social healthcare programs offered by the local public governance, and performing monthly breast self-exams as an issue associated with social education. As social-media activities achieve scale of returns over a period, the challenges of the company may center less around justifying funding and more on organizational issues such as developing the right processes and governance structure and identifying clear roles for all involved in social-media strategy. Managers can identify the functions, touch points, and goals of social-media activities, and craft approaches to measure their impact and manage their risks. However, companies may need to drive internal discussions on how to lead and to learn from social networks, competitors, and young consumers to stay competitive in the marketplace (Rajagopal 2013).

Most developing nations have promulgated comprehensive public policies to streamline corporate governance on implementation of sustainability-driven business model in all industries. Public policies are focusing on macroeconomic disruption due to sustainability issues in developing economies (Béal 2015). Therefore, large companies are developing alliances with local governments on public–private partnerships (PPP) in implementing sustainability norms and enhancing social value. The PPP initiatives in various geodemographic sectors have generated social awareness among people and inculcated the environmentally conscious consumption in the society. The core elements of crowdfunded business projects constitute stakeholders, society, innovation and technology, macroeconomic factors, sustainability, and corporate governance. Crowd-sourcing or collective intelligence has emerged as a dynamic tool in the business ecosystem today, which is supported by the stakeholders. They support companies in cocreation and coevolution process with stakeholders through social interaction, social innovations, and social governance. Ecosystem of crowd-based businesses that are linked with the sustainability goals drives public–private entrepreneurship (both upstream and downstream collaborations) to meet the sustainable development goals through social and frugal innovations. Upstream collaboration refers to strategic alliances with national or international firms to have regional or global focus of business, while downstream collaborations are associated with the social business and community governance. Taxonomy of leadership and employee engagement largely drives the corporate governance practices as central to the business ecosystem (Rajagopal 2021). In the context of an industry, business ecosystem is a community comprising various levels of interdependent firms that tend to coevolve in an ongoing business cycle and constantly renew their business configurations. The business cycle of a firm is largely affected by political, economic, social, technological, and legal subsystems. In view of the ecosystem discussed previously, the coevolutionary process of business modeling consists of covision, co-designing, and cocreation as the domains of the activities (Liu and Rong 2015). Consumers also play a significant role in the innovation subsystem by cocreating products that add value to the social sustainability. End-users share insights on low-cost innovations and the possible ways of their utility with the consumer communities. The consumer-led social innovations are supported by public policies and encouraged through the nongovernmental organizations and public–private participation. End-users contribute to the innovation processes by contributing to the design perspectives and stimulating demand of the innovative product. Thus, stakeholders, corporate managers, and policymakers remain apprehensive about the potential of end-users driving sustainable innovation (Nielsen 2020).

Implementation and governance of sustainability-based business models are shared through public–private partnerships. In addition, stakeholder-driven governance forms such as cooperatives, public private partnerships, or social businesses help companies transcend narrow profit-maximizing models. The business models are analyzed from a sustainability perspective to overcome the economic, social, and technological bias of sustainability approaches. Accordingly, business governance leading to performance with purpose is designed in improving social sector and operates through interactive business models categorically in geodemographic market segments (Sánchez and Ricart 2010). Business transformation in consumer-centric companies evolves over the years in reference to value-based governance. The necessity of creating hybrid business models infuses with local cultures and practices in global markets, leveraging strategic partnerships by encouraging cocreation with consumers. The community creation model in managing renewable business projects across the downstream market comprising rural household and farm and nonfarm sectors functions more as social governance than a corporate venture. The governance mechanism for managing green energy projects in the rural areas lies between the hierarchy-based (closed) mechanism and the market-based (open) systems. Social behavior is built by attaining social needs through stakeholder governance and effective social governance. Sustainability projects lead to success as social behavior is strengthened by perceived social beliefs, values, and community consciousness. Psychosocial behavior, which is supported by the stakeholder education and experience, emotions, and motivations, also contributes to the social behavior in general. Positive impact of public governance based on the public policies on sustainable goods and services sets the consumption behavior among the stakeholders. The social leadership and working group on the sustainable projects not only generate awareness on the eco-innovation and technologies but also boost social motivation among the stakeholders to adapt to the ecological products and services.

Inclusive Marketing-Mix

Implementation of effective marketing strategy is a "building-block" exercise which requires perfect coordination among various elements of marketing-mix and associated attributes like emotions, validity of decisions, and consumer value. Such architecture of marketing strategies helps companies in developing a brilliant breakthrough of their products and services in the competitive marketplace. Companies have experimented several ways in the past century to develop and implement a successful marketing strategy. Marketing strategies are developed by the companies to fit into the organizational design of the companies. Design of a marketing organization is founded on the structural variables, organizational resources including human capital and finance, capabilities and competencies, and the workplace culture. The performance of marketing strategies varies for the companies with different organizational designs representing prospectors, analyzers, low-cost defenders, and competitive differentiation-oriented company policies. However, marketing-mix practices can be modified in reference to the culture, strategy formation process, market-focused strategic organizational behaviors, and marketing control systems of the marketing organization (Slater et al. 2010).

Most consumer-centric companies work with dynamic marketing-mix, as strategies often need to be revised either by introducing ad hoc elements of marketing strategies, or by laying emphasis on specific marketing-mix elements to develop marketing strategies specific to the geodemographic segments. The widespread adoption of marketing technology driving e-commerce trends and social media leveraging peer interactions to share their consumption experiences have dramatically altered the set of products consumers compare before making a purchase decision. Marketing through social channels in the 21st century has succeeded in connecting consumers with companies, brands, and destinations by highlighting peer evaluations, consumer preferences, and motivations toward buying decisions. However, the contribution of marketing technology in establishing both product and customer interconnectedness across markets prompts companies to make the dynamic decision based on the market competition trends. The dynamic marketing decisions often develop inconsistencies in the consumer policies of the company and affect the deliverables of the brands (Dass and Kumar 2014).

Successful companies are selective toward systematically developing strategies to create and lead new markets. Marketing-mix strategies need to be appropriately designed for acquiring new consumers, and retaining those existing, by providing competitive leverage and customer value. Developing marketing strategies for new customers with unfamiliar brands is challenging for the companies. An appropriate marketing-mix also guides companies to minimize cost–time–risk convergence in marketing and optimize market share and profitability. The opportunity to create and dominate a new market offers the prospect of working with right marketing-mix to gain competitive leverage in the marketplace and enhance the scope of business performance and profitability. However, most consumer-centric companies like FedEx, AT&T, and GlaxoSmithKline chose the path to develop consumer awareness about brands and their associated values to integrate delivery of products, customer interfaces, and support systems (Meyer 2002).

Marketing-mix adopted by the consumer-centric companies is largely technology-oriented, as each element of the marketing-mix is configured with the requirements of growing marketing technology. Effective use of digital space in business has made e-commerce and m-commerce more popular over the conventional telemarketing strategies of the 20th century. Mobile marketing and visual merchandizing with the help of online product simulations have boosted the product innovation and market competition. The digital marketing approaches have emerged as an increasingly dominant component of a firm's overall promotional strategy. The involvement of social media in sharing experiences of the consumers as an intangible tool has generated strong psychodynamic effects empowering consumer to govern the performance of products and services. The importance of this element in marketing-mix can be seen as the extent and quality of engagement of consumers on digital platforms, time spent on mobile media, managing consumer forums, and participating in public blogs on Internet, number of searches, and direct and indirect referral to promote sales. However, the effectiveness of marketing technology needs to be improved by monitoring the shifts in "consumer–convenience–cost–community" metrics representing the significance of 4Cs in marketing strategies.

The emergence of e-commerce has prompted consumer-centric companies to adapt to "direct-to-customer" (DTC) distribution strategy. This strategy has been successful over the years as it helps companies in minimizing the cost, time, and risk (CTR) effects in managing distribution. Lowering the CTR effects results in increasing the consumer value, brand loyalty, market share, and profitability of the company. The DTC strategy, therefore, can be defined as a digital sales channel evolved as convenience shopping outlet without a fixed retail location. Such technology-led distribution strategy is built by leveraging the consumers' engagement in social media and power of Internet shopping. The DTC practices are embedded in the social media, as marketing through the Facebook has become cost-effective for the companies on one hand, while it also provides psychodynamics among the consumers on the other. However, the challenge lies in providing the benefits of face-to-face selling, augmented by social media. The DTC marketing today has a streamlined distribution system through the third-party suppliers and using the inventory system owned by the e-commerce companies like Amazon and Alibaba. The DTC distribution management involves social media as a driver of CTR-associated distribution strategy. In this strategy, companies improve customer relationships by developing skills in carefully listening, documenting, and responding to their concerns. The DTC transactions are done with transparency, consumer confidence, and within the ethical organizational cultures, which expands consumer communities and enhances consumer value (Ferrell and Ferrell 2012).

Products in the contemporary marketplace are consumer-driven and are developed as a solution to the consumer needs. The intangible factor of perceived use value and tangible preference of consumers determining the value for money of products governs the decision-making process for products among consumers. Products with high perceived value and longevity and delivering expected value for money stay as top-of-mind products among consumers. Therefore, in a dynamic competition, companies periodically offer programs on improvements of product designs to deliver continuous improvement in the product quality.

Consumer-centric companies like Apple, IKEA, Procter and Gamble, and General Electric consider that both design and marketing strategies are important tools in creating product preference, perceived use value, and deeper emotional value for the consumers. In the context of changing global business trends, relationship-based customer management is integrated with the product management strategies to drive emotional values among consumers. Product attractiveness is largely driven by product design, competitive leverages, and consumer preferences. Hence, most consumer-centric companies are engaged in cocreating product designs. Companies engage consumers to share their experience, while the consumers offer solutions to the companies in the form of products designs, services, and expected values. Companies deliver these cocreated tangibles in the competitive marketplace. Product differentiation is another major challenge for consumer-centric companies to stay ahead of marketplace competition. Most companies believe that successful product differentiation allows the consumer brands to enter mass market in the emerging markets (Rajagopal 2019).

In the increasing market competition today, promotional strategies of products and services have become one of the principal drivers for the success of business performance. Today, the advertising strategies experience a facelift from conventional to digital manifestations engaging consumers to cocreate promotions of products and services. Most advertisements of consumer products in the contemporary business are based on user-generated contents and consumer experience shared on the social media. The promotional strategies are evaluated by the companies in reference to its impact on volume of sales, market share, and their contribution to the profit specific to the products and services. The promotional strategies of consumer-centric companies have become a large and growing part of marketing budgets of companies worldwide. Among the fashion-oriented brands, promotions are largely driven by the word-of-mouth and interactions on social media with other consumers. Sales promotions need to be reviewed in reference to economic viability, informational aspect that consumers use to make purchase decisions, and affective aspects that help in generating consumer experience (Raghubir et al. 2004). The elements of marketing mix that are influenced by the inclusivity in business are exhibited in Figure 3.2.

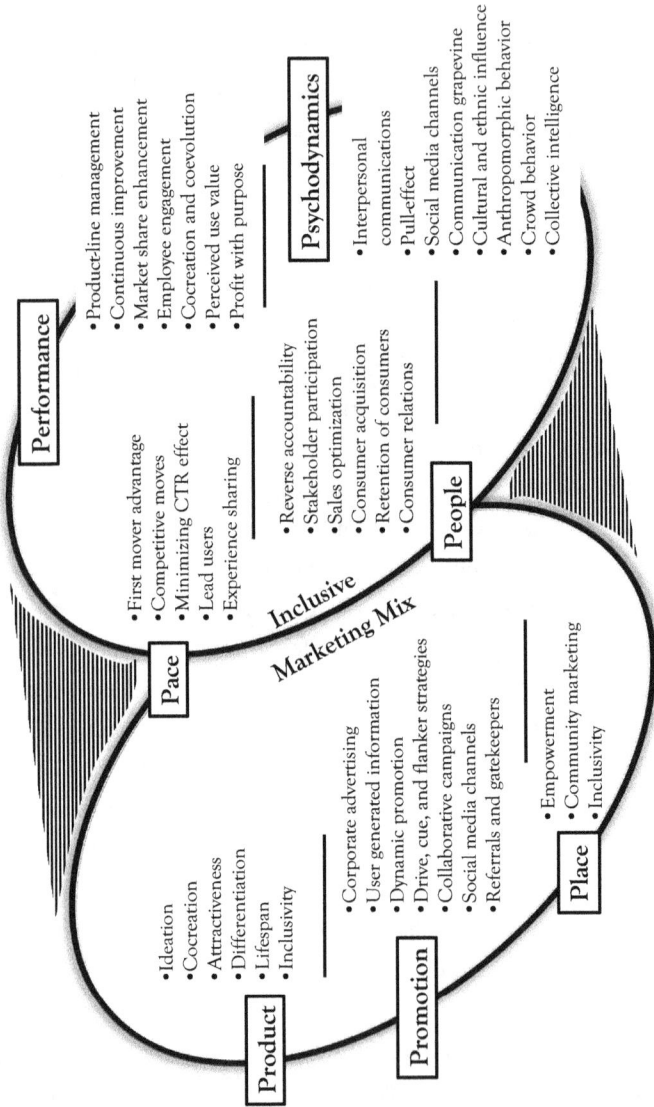

Figure 3.2 Inclusivity effects in marketing mix

Source: Author

The influence of inclusivity on marketing strategy focuses on the people atop other business elements to drive performance with a social perspective as illustrated in Figure 3.2. The involvement of stakeholders and customers drives collaborative ideation and cocreation process in new product development, while their engagement highly influences the promotion of products. The user-generated contents, collective intelligence, creativity, and the role of referrals and gatekeepers widely support the advertising and communication strategies in the inclusive businesses. Farmers play significant role in agribusiness in determining the minimum support price in the food grain procurement process in the developing countries. The inclusivity in pricing in the agribusiness sector is also supported by the public policies in these countries. Inclusivity in distribution and community marketing has been experimented by the Hindustan Unilever Limited (HUL) in India and other developing countries through the empowerment of rural men and women in marketing the products of HUL within rural neighborhoods. The Mary Kay Cosmetics, a women-centric American company, is also coevolving its business by engaging women in marketing its products to improve household income and quality of life through inclusivity in business. These strategies evidence inclusivity in distribution of products within the community and at the BOP. The first mover advantage (pace) is backed by the experience sharing of stakeholders and key business partners on social and digital media channels, while reverse accountability of stakeholders ensures performance of the company embedding the objective of profit with purpose. In addition, the psychodynamics (consumer-to-consumer business approach) helps in generating pull effect in the market by augmenting the demand for the products of the company. The pull effect helps the company to lower the costs of marketing, stay customer-centric, and increase profit over time.

Etymologically, "pace" indicates consistent and continuous speed in moving things. In the context of business, pace illustrates the marketing strategies for going ahead of competitors. Most companies in the competitive marketplace struggle to gain the first mover advantage, increase market share, and augment profit. Companies, as first movers, also spend more resources to attract consumers and position their brands, which tends to lower the profit rate. However, efficient companies try to minimize the cost, time, and risk (CTR) factors in launching and delivering products in the marketplace. Many companies believe that the first company in a new product category gets a significant breakthrough in the markets and gets long-lasting benefits. However, it does not happen always. To ensure the advantages from the pace strategy, companies should monitor the gradual evolution in both the technology and the right opportunity to move in the market, which could provide a first mover by influencing the consumers and creating demand in the neighboring markets. Such market situation might offer a dominant position in the market. For example, robotic vacuum cleaners launched by the "i-Robot" Company had expected the first mover advantages over the initial period as a new technology supported home-cleaning gadget (Rajagopal 2019).

However, when the technology is changing rapidly, it is hard to get a first mover advantage for a company. Therefore, the new entrants should manage the CTR factors by deploying resources rationally and aiming at the long-term advantage by developing convergence between the technology and use value of products. Apple Company had faced low response toward the first mover advantage for its *i-Pod* product in developing countries when launched against the Walkman brand of Sony. Often, a company with limited resources must settle for a short-term benefit. However, when the market is stagnated with consumer preferences but the changing technology is pushing innovation in the products, the first-mover advantages may occur for the companies which tend to deploy increasing resources in product advertising, promotions, and consumer services (Suarez and Lanzolla 2005). Companies moving to new markets should carefully analyze the business environment and assess resources, and determine which type of first-mover advantage is achievable in view of minimizing the CTR factors.

People in the marketing-mix constitute front-liners in markets, who manage sales of products and services. Selling is an art largely associated with the behavioral skills of the sale personnel of a sales organization. In a competitive marketplace, selling is performed using scientific methods of product presentation, advertising, and various approaches drawn to take the customer into confidence. A firm begins to sell its products in a competitive marketplace, thrives continuously on acquiring new customers, and launches new product lines or services in order to gain competitive advantage, retain the existing customers, enhance customer value, and gain competitive lead in the market. To compete in a dynamic and inter- active marketplace environment, firms must transform their focus from just selling the products and services to value-added sales management, to maximize customer lifetime value, and to encourage repeat sales. Hence, firms should ensure that products and services offered by salespeople must be made subservient to customer relationships. The new generation sales management strategies grow out of the basic marketing-mix strate- gies comprising product, price, place, and promotion. The front-liners strategies need not only to focus on enhancing the volume of sales but also to serve customers for generating long-term customer loyalty. Sales effectiveness is developed through cost-control and customer value aug- mentation process. It has been observed that selling process has changed over time, and most firms have adopted customer-centric selling process because of increase in the market competition due to fast penetration of global firms (Rajagopal 2010).

Conceptualizing sales strategy and examining its impact on sales force and firm performance have been addressed in this book in reference to sales force design, managing sale territories, industrial selling, account management, sales force automation, recruitment and compensation. Sales strategy can be made operational as a multidimensional construct in reference to customer segmentation, targeting, customer prioritization, framing relationship objectives, developing selling models, and selling through new routes to market (Panagopoulos and Avlonitis 2010). Efficiency in delivering sales and services has been driven by globaliza- tion and the growth of technology over time, but the fundamentals of sales have not radically changed. Conventional wisdom among salespeo- ple still overrides the sales automation process in some cases. However, the principal task in sales activity calls for the ways to maximize their relationship benefits in reference to acquiring customers, settling price, offering convenience, and delivering postsales service. Though virtual shopping is observed to be a fast-growing channel, the Internet has just added another layer of convenience to customers in an innovative manner (Maruca 1999).

Salespeople in a competitive marketplace are considered as human capital of the organization who directly contribute toward the generation of revenue. The sales and profit contribution of the salespeople should be accounted as their per capita productivity. Companies need to develop a system that allows sales managers to monitor and evaluate the human capital periodically on the basis of cost-productivity metrics, both to predict individual performance and to guide organizations' investments in people. The principal drivers for measuring the productivity of salespeople include leadership practices, employee engagement, knowledge accessibility, workforce optimization, and customer relationship management competencies (Bassi and McMurrer 2007). Effective sales strategies have a direct bearing on possessing the relative brand equity and growth of the business. Sales strategies are the directional statements that need to be converted into a step-by-step plan of action for effective plan implementation. The strategic sales directions have four options expressed by 4As—arena, advantage, access, and activities. The arena may be defined as competitive prospecting of the target consumers or key accounts through an appropriate scale of information flow, advantage appropriation, and customer relations. Marketplace arena is a challenging ground for the salespeople to show their performance and establish their lead among competitors. For example, traditionally, sales force of multinational companies targets consumers in the premium segment, while a plethora of domestic companies look for prospecting low-end consumer segment, often unprofitably (Orit et al. 2007).

Grapevine is an emerging informal channel of business communication, and a critical element in creating tangible interactions among consumers in a competitive marketplace. The grapevine effect is contributed by the social media through word-of-mouth that stretches throughout the market irrespective of the various measures taken by the firms to build their brand and competitive posture. Grapevine develops psychodynamics among consumers by sharing various consumer experiences on the firms, products, or services. The consumer perceptions lead to positive or negative effects of the grapevine in reference to the extent of the satisfaction or dissatisfaction accrued on any incidence of business negotiation or product experience. Grapevine channels carry information rapidly and spread it faster than the formal business communication of the firms. There are many types of grapevines that are developed in various niches grown on emotion, sensitivity, personality, assumptions, experiences, and social conventions. Informal channels grown on these cognitive determinants create a sense of accord among the consumers in the marketplace who share and discuss their views with each other. Thus, grapevine helps in developing group cohesiveness and serves as an emotional supportive value in putting forth the consumer voice in the market (Rajagopal 2013).

Positive psychodynamics among consumers creates pull-effect for specific brands in the market. The pull-effect generates high consumer demand, which benefit companies in increasing market share and profit by reducing the marketing costs. Such costs for brands are spread across advertisements, in-store promotions, price discounts, and point-of-sales incentives to the consumers. The psychodynamics also generates referrals and brand advocacy behavior among consumers, which helps companies acquire new consumers at relatively low cost. Most firms involving social media as a marketing communication channel tap the knowledge and expertise of consumers for mutual benefit and for brand building process more than a traditional knowledge management approach where people dump their information in a giant database that nobody reads. Such firms can create an environment where they go through the peer-to-peer collaboration. Emerging firms may initially build very small collaborative tools that could enable their peer communication design to kick-off the consumer-company collaboration process and to get experience in understanding how it provides mutual benefits (Rajagopal 2013).

Case Studies: Inclusivity and Corporate Social Responsibility

Inclusivity in business and corporate social responsibility (CSR) has symbiotic relationship. Most companies have experienced the success of CSR programs by effectively engaging stakeholders in the concept of development and implementation process. CSR programs with inclusive philosophy can achieve the social and environmental goals. In addition, voluntary participation of people and involvement of government in identifying social problems, needs, and potential solution help companies to implement CSR programs successfully at the grassroots. Thus, CSR programs can be cocreated and coevolved with the engagement of stakeholders, social leaders, and government to serve the social development objectives and making profit with purpose. Stakeholders play a significant role in enabling social ecosystem for enabling CSR activities with the support of public policies and socio-political leadership across developing economies. Consequently, the inclusivity in CSR is encouraged to cocreate and coevolve environmental policies and to support global movements that promote CSR (Branco et al. 2018).

The CSR is considered by the companies as an investment toward gaining confidence and loyalty of the stakeholder through design-to-society and design-to-value initiatives. Therefore, the CSR programs are planned specifically to cater to the social development needs, supervised carefully, and evaluated regularly to optimize the benefits to the stakeholders. The CSR programs contribute to the primary development needs of the society through the collective efforts, planning, implementation, monitoring, and evaluation. The perceived benefits of CSR programs by the stakeholders significantly contribute to the corporate reputation. Besides the corporate reputation, the CSR programs also attract, retain, and motivate stakeholders and employees to work collectively on the social, economic, and sustainability initiatives. From the perspectives of social requirements, a good reputation of the company implementing CSR programs increases the value of its brand portfolios. As companies are adopting rapidly the inclusive business environment and using the social and cultural goods to implement the CSR programs, the social values are increasingly influenced by the stakeholder participation. Multinational enterprises face lack of clarity in social leadership and community initiatives. In addition, transparencies in social governance in CSR programs also affect the community drive toward implementing such programs with social objectives involving stakeholders. Nike has involved stakeholders and customer in the design thinking process. At Nike, product design and innovation are at the core of the creative process by including employees and stakeholders in ideation of new products. The talent strategy centers across destinations helps in exploring and developing diverse talent through cocreation and coevolution involving stakeholders and customers.

CSR has been conceived largely as a voluntary corporate commitment with implicit obligations imposed on a company to meet the expectations of the society through inclusive corporate behavior. CSR has emerged as a way of promoting social benefits that cover both the legal framework and social conventions. With the increasing effect of globalization, companies are now less constrained by the basic socioeconomic order of the society than in the past due to flexible laws and standards. The CSR is largely influenced by the crowd behavior and collective intelligence, which motivate companies to evaluate the CSR programs proposed on crowd platforms. Accordingly, the companies can conceive CSR as a long-range plan of action (Falck and Heblich 2007).

ITC Agribusiness India

The agribusiness division of ITC is one of largest exporters of agricultural commodities and has opted the *e-choupal* business model.[2] E-Choupal is conceived as a more efficient communication center and supply chain that delivers value to customers on a sustainable basis. This model has been specially designed to meet the challenges of marginal and small farmers in marketing their produce. The involvement of middlemen and intermediaries and weak market infrastructure in the agriculture sector have deprived farmers from marketing their produce at better prices. This *e-choupal* program has empowered farmers, raised rural income, and developed the rural ecosystem. This program also aimed at re-designing the procurement practices of soy, tobacco, shrimp, wheat, and other cropping material required by the company. The model has created highly profitable distribution and product design channel for the enterprise. ITC procures major food grains directly from farmers that results in eliminating middlemen and save cost in warehousing and delays. This practice has also led to consistency and predictability in the supply chain. The use of informational technology has been promoted in *e-choupal,* and as an inclusive business experiment, the company has invested in setting up of

---

[2] Digital forum of farmers to discuss farming and agribusiness-related topics. For details on e-Choupal program of ITC, see www.itcportal.com/businesses/agri-business/e-choupal.aspx.

broad band digital networks and logistics even in remote areas to enable farmers to receive updated information on pricing and procurement logistics. This has brought transparency, increased access to information, catalyzed rural transformation, while enabling efficiencies and low-cost distribution of food grains that make the system profitable and sustainable. Farmers are provided with critical information and relevant knowledge on farm productivity, prices, and markets through the *e-choupal* digital infrastructure. In addition, farmers are also provided access to quality inputs to augment productivity. The company has set up integrated rural service, which provides multiple services under single-window delivery system. Sustainable nonfarm livelihoods opportunities for over 40,000 rural women through microenterprises with financial support also have been provided by the company as a part of *e-choupal.* Inclusive business cultures emphasize agility, open-mindedness, and collective actions to cocreate and innovate services to enhance the stakeholder values. The power of community and culture should be aligned with inclusive business strategy for each stakeholder-oriented business project. However, the efficacy of employees and stakeholders' engagement provides sustainable business environment by reducing the impact of cost, time, and risk factors (Cheng and Groysberg 2021).

The e-choupal inclusive business model economically empowers the marginal and small farmers who have low risk-taking ability, low investment, low productivity, weak market orientation, low value addition, and low income. Such economic conditions make the agribusiness an uncompetitive enterprise for marketing and small farmers. Such a market-led business model can enhance the competitiveness of marginal and small farmers and trigger a virtuous cycle of higher productivity, higher incomes, enlarged capacity for farmer risk management, larger investments, and higher quality and productivity. The inclusive business model of *e-choupal* serves as an information pool, logistics management, lowering risk, and bridging financing gaps. Real-time information and customized knowledge provided by *e-choupal* enhance the ability of farmers to take decisions and align their farm output with market demand. The aggregation of the demand for farm inputs from individual farmers gives them access to high-quality inputs from established and reputed manufacturers at fair prices. As a direct marketing channel, it virtually linked to the regulated agricultural marketing system for price discovery and eliminated wasteful intermediation and multiple handling. Consequently, this program helps in significantly reducing transaction costs.

Shakti Experiment: Hindustan Unilever Limited, India

Hindustan Unilever Limited (HUL), a multinational consumer product, has exhibited the corporate excellence by developing inclusive business model not only to create social value but also to market its products at the BOP market segment. Implementing the inclusive business model, the company has focused on empowering rural women economically and creating social value by providing opportunities to improve their social value and quality of life. The inclusive business activities and initiatives of the company are aligned with their business operations and practices. Of various projects of HUL, *Project Shakti*[3] has been able to deliver and create a positive impact on the people at the BOP, which provided substantial economic empowerment to the women stakeholders. *Project Shakti* enables rural women in villages across India to nurture an entrepreneurial mindset and become financially independent. Their role enables to sell HUL products to the small retail outlets in their immediate village as well as directly to the households within the community. This project was launched in 2001, with an objective to empower underprivileged rural women by training them in health and hygiene, and allowing them to undertake income-generation activities such as distribution and retailing of HUL consumer brands.

The women, known as *Vanis* (communicators), have been engaged in selling soap, shampoo, and other personal care products of HUL through social forums such as schools and village gatherings. *Project Shakti* entrepreneurs, who are commonly known as *Shakti Ammas* (empowered

---

[3] For details on the Shakti experiment of Hindustan Unilever Limited toward adapting to the diversity and inclusivity in business, see www.hul.co.in/planet-and-society/case-studies/enhancing-livelihoods-through-project-shakti/ (Retrieved on March 12, 2022).

women in local dialect and ethnic expressions), reach out to over four million households across 1,65,000 villages spread over different states in India. These households form a new market for HUL where its products are sold, generating revenue for the company, while simultaneously improving the per capita income. This model expanded the outreach of products of the company and employment opportunities to the rural women. HUL also promotes skill development by providing training in sales practices, financial knowledge, and bookkeeping to help them become microentrepreneurs. The company had increased the number of *Shakti* entrepreneurs to 75,000 in 2015 in which women entrepreneurs were complemented by 48,000 *Shaktimaans* (empowered men in local dialect and ethnic expressions), who are typically the husbands or brothers of the women entrepreneurs. *Shaktimaans* sell HUL's products on bicycles in surrounding villages, covering a larger area than *Shakti Ammas* used to cover on foot. At the end of 2020, we have nearly 1,36,000 Shakti entrepreneurs spread across 18 states. *Project Shakti* has helped generate income by selling our products and has created a great impact on the livelihoods of women.

A team of Rural Sales Promoters coach *Shakti Ammas* in rural India by familiarizing them with HUL products and the simple corporate practice of sales. The skill development includes basics of sales management and soft skills of negotiation and communication. This project embraces HUL's philosophy of *Doing Well by Doing Good,* a philosophy that has been extended even during the pandemic of COVID-19. To ensure uninterrupted supply of stock to women entrepreneurs, the regional sales team of the company and distributors implemented innovative ways of demand capture and fulfilment for the *Shakti* Channel. The rural salesmen were also provided hygiene kits, were trained on best hygiene practices, and a COVID-19 care package was included in their medical insurance policy. The rural salesmen extended their support to both men and women entrepreneurs by going beyond their traditional roles of capturing demand, driving awareness on handwashing, and maintaining proper hygiene. Experiencing the *Project Shakti* Model similar programs has been launched by the company across Sri Lanka, Pakistan, Ethiopia, Egypt, and Columbia. And so, the journey of *Project Shakti* continues beyond 2021.

Sodexo: Food Management Services

Diversity and inclusion of stakeholders have become a new business practice, as the benefits of having diverse talent in a team are growing continuously. The diversity-and-inclusion policy helps to create inclusive businesses and collective working environment. Sodexo, a food and management services provider,[4] has diversity in hiring strategy across gender, age, and sexual orientation. The company focused on gender balance in its overall business strategy over the years. Sodexo was included in the 2020 Bloomberg Gender Equality Index, which tracks the financial performance of companies committed to gender equality. Sodexo makes conscious efforts to create a quality and lifestyle difference in everyday actions. The company focuses on providing nutrition and well-being, and delivers the corporate social responsibilities to support sustainability and improving the social health and value. Sodexo ensures the right value spread across the stakeholders without discrimination. Accordingly, the company works with suppliers, affiliates and organizations that share similar corporate vision, and strive to promote the long-term empowerment of minorities. The company embeds the philosophy of continuous improvement in programs and pursuing toward goal of an inclusive culture.

The inclusivity program of Sodexo has a flagship activity, which is focusing on *stop hunger* program at the BOP, popularly floated through the employees and volunteers. Stop Hunger has been acting in the society as an inclusive instrument for over 25 years. Drawing upon the vital support of Sodexo, this program aims at sustainably eradicating hunger and support women's empowerment. The beneficiaries continue to hope for a better quality of life and are committed to tackling hunger alongside local and international nongovernmental partners. *Stop Hunger* is a collective action program and has distributed 8.5 million meals along with its volunteers, donors, and founding partner Sodexo. In addition to food aid, Stop Hunger has provided effective support to 200 food banks, some of which are members of the Global Food Banking Network and

---

[4] This is a French food services and facilities management company with headquartered in Paris. The U.S. head office of the company is located at Gaithersburg, Maryland.

nongovernmental organizations. This program continued to provide support in France[5] (Restos du Coeur charity), United States (Sodexo), Great Britain (FareShare), and Australia (Foodbank). Sodexo has also extended support in Brazil, Colombia, Indonesia, the Philippines, and India, where the communities suffered from business lockdowns and the second wave of the pandemic.

Globally, inclusive businesses are being recognized as an important driver for development. More companies are realizing the BOP market segment as profit-with-purpose opportunity. Such business philosophy helps the companies with inclusive business models to design and implement innovative solutions with strategic business and social welfare perspectives. However, inclusive businesses continue to face several barriers in scaling and replicating their success such as lack of access to finance, absence of trained human resources, and weak supply chain linkages. Besides, in most developing countries, the inclusive business companies have underdeveloped support ecosystem to overcome critical market gaps.

References

Barton, D., and M. Wiseman. 2014. "Focusing Capital on the Long Term." *Harvard Business Review* 92, no. 1/2, pp. 44–51.

Bassi, L., and D. McMurrer. 2007. "Maximizing Your Return on People." *Harvard Business Review* 85, no. 3, pp. 115–123.

Branco, M.C., C. Delgado, and C. Marques. 2018. "How Do Sustainability Reports From the Nordic and the Mediterranean European Countries Compare?" *Review of Management Science* 12, pp. 917–936.

Béal, V. 2015. "Selective Public Policies: Sustainability and Neoliberal Urban Restructuring." *Environment and Urbanization* 27, no. 1, pp. 303–316.

Chambers, R. 1994. "The Origins and Practice of Participatory Rural Appraisal." *World Development* 22, no. 7, pp. 953–969.

Cheng, J.Y., and B. Groysberg. June 2021. "Research: What Inclusive Companies Have in Common." *Harvard Business Review*.

Dass, M., and S. Kumar. 2014. "Bringing Product and Consumer Ecosystems to the Strategic Forefront." *Business Horizons* 57, no. 2, pp. 225–234.

---

[5] Names in parentheses belong to the organizations associated with *Stop Hunger* program in the respective countries.

Elezi, F., D. Resch, I.D. Tommelein, and U. Lindemann. 2013. *Improving Organizational Design and Diagnosis by Supporting Viable System Model Application With Structural Complexity Management,* In E. Scheurmann, M. Maurer, D. Schmidt, and U. Lindemann. (eds.), pp. 113–140. Reducing Risk in Innovation. Oxford: William Andrew Publishing.

Falck, O., and S. Heblich. 2007. "Corporate Social Responsibility: Doing Well by Doing Good." *Business Horizons* 50, no. 3, pp. 247–254.

Ferrell, L., and O.C. Ferrell. 2012. "Redirecting Direct Selling: High-Touch Embraces High-Tech." *Business Horizons* 55, no. 3, pp. 273–281.

Ingram, P. 2021. *The Forgotten Dimension of Diversity.* Harvard Business Review Digital Article, Cambridge, MA: Harvard Business School.

Jalilianhasanpour, R., S. Asadollahi, and D.M. Yousem. 2021. "Creating Joy in the Workplace." *European Journal of Radiology.* 145, (in Press). https://doi.org/10.1016/j.ejrad.2021.110019

Khanna, P. 2012. *The Rise of Hybrid Governance.* New York, NY: McKinsey & Company.

Knowles, H.P., and B.O. Saxberg. 1988. "Organizational Leadership of Planned and Unplanned Change: A Systems Approach to Organizational Viability." *Futures* 20, no. 3, pp. 252–265.

Liu, S., W. Xiao, C. Fang, X. Zhang, and J. Lin. 2020. "Social Support, Belongingness, and Value Co-Creation Behaviors in Online Health Communities." *Telematics and Informatics* 50, (in press). https://doi.org/10.1016/j.tele.2020.101398

Liu, G., and K. Rong. 2015. "The Nature of the Co-Evolutionary Process: Complex Product Development in the Mobile Computing Industry's Business Ecosystem." *Group & Organization Management* 40, no. 6, pp. 809–842.

Meyer, P. 2002. "Proven Strategies for New Market Mastery." *Business Horizons* 45, no. 3, pp. 6–10.

Maruca, R.F. 1999. "Retailing: Confronting the Challenges That Face Bricks-and-Mortar Stores." *Harvard Business Review* 77, no. 4, pp. 159–168.

Nielsen, K.R. 2020. "Policymakers' Views on Sustainable End-User Innovation: Implications for Sustainable Innovation." *Journal of Cleaner Production* 254. doi.org/10.1016/j.jclepro.2020.120030

Orit, G., L. Philip, and V. Till. 2007. "Battle in China's Good-Enough Market." *Harvard Business Review* 85, no. 9, pp. 80–89.

Osterwalder, A., and Y. Pigneur. 2010. *Business Model Generation: A Handbook for Visionaries, Game Changers, and Challengers.* NJ: John Wiley & Sons.

Panagopoulos, N.G., and G.J. Avlonitis. 2010. "Performance Implications of Sales Strategy: The Moderating Effects of Leadership and Environment." *International Journal of Research in Marketing* 27, no. 1, pp. 46–57.

Pound, J. 2015. "Promise of the Governed Corporation." *Harvard Business Review* 3, no. 2, pp. 89–98.

Raghubir, P., J.J. Inman, and H. Grande. 2004. "Three Faces of Consumer Promotions." *California Management Review* 46, no. 4, pp. 23–42.

Rajagopal. 2010. *Sales Dynamics: Thinking Outside the Box.* Hauppauge. New York, NY: Nova Science Publishers Inc.

Rajagopal. 2013. *Managing Social Media and Consumerism: The Grapevine Effect in Competitive Markets.* Basingstoke, UK: Palgrave Macmillan.

Rajagopal. 2019. *Contemporary Marketing Strategy: Analyzing Consumer Behavior to Drive Managerial Decision Making.* New York, NY: Palgrave Macmillan.

Rajagopal. 2021. *Crowd-Based Business Models—Using Collective Intelligence for Market Competitiveness.* New York, NY: Palgrave Macmillan.

Schön, D.A. 2017. *The Reflective Practitioner: How Professionals Think in Action.* Philadelphia, PA: Taylor and Francis.

Sánchez, P., and J. Ricart. 2010. "Business Model Innovation and Sources of Value Creation in Low-Income Markets." *European Management Review* 7, no. 1, pp. 138–154.

Scaliza, J.A.A., D. Jugend, C.J.C. Jabbour, H. Latan, F. Armellini, D. Twigg, and D.F. Andrade. 2022. "Relationships Among Organizational Culture, Open Innovation, Innovative Ecosystems, and Performance of Firms: Evidence From an Emerging Economy Context." *Journal of Business Research* 140, pp. 264–279.

Senge, P.M. 1990. "Leader's New Work: Building Learning Organizations." *MIT Sloan Management Review* 32, no. 1, pp. 7–23.

Shore, L.M., J.N. Cleveland, and D. Sanchez. 2018. "Inclusive Workplaces: A Review and Model." *Human Resource Management Review* 28, no. 2, pp. 176–189.

Slater. S.F., E.M. Olson, and G.T.M. Hult. 2010. "Worried About Strategy Implementation? Don't Overlook Marketing's Role." *Business Horizons* 53, no. 5, pp. 469–479.

Sokhi, J., J. Desborough, N. Norris, and D.J. Wright. 2020. "Learning From Community Pharmacists' Initial Experiences of a Workplace-Based Training Program." *Currents in Pharmacy Teaching and Learning* 12, no. 8, pp. 932–939.

Suarez, F.F., and G. Lanzolla. 2005. "Half-Truth of First-Mover Advantage." *Harvard Business Review* 83, no. 4, pp. 121–127.

Subramanian, G. 2015. "Corporate Governance 2.0." *Harvard Business Review* 93, no. 3, pp. 96–105.

Teece, D.J. 2010. "Business Models, Business Strategy and Innovation." *Long Range Planning* 43, no. 2–3, pp. 172–194.

Thomke, S., and M. Sinha. 2010. *The Dabbawala System: On-Time Delivery, Every Time.* Boston, MA: Harvard Business School Press.

CHAPTER 4

Continuous Learning

Continuous learning has grown as the vital process in social- and customer-centric businesses and analyzes the success and failure experiences in doing business with people (Lopez et al. 2006). The participatory business appraisal as a new concept has been discussed as a continuous learning tool by engaging customers, stake holders, and crowd within the business ecosystem. Participatory appraisals are used as a driver to actions research in resolving social issues and analyzing the cultural, biological, and legal perspectives to promote customer-centric businesses on a social scale. This chapter discusses the broad perspectives of continuous learning and its effects on organizational culture. The role of organizational learning on design thinking and systems thinking is also discussed in this chapter. The process of developing organizational mission and vision has also been discussed in the in the context of organizational learning and thinking philosophies. The two case studies on Mukamas, a Finnish learning agglomerate, and General Electric's (GE) bottom-up communications endorse the concepts of continuous learning, design thinking, and systems thinking that are discussed in this chapter.

Continuous Learning and Organizational Culture

Organizational learning is a continuous process which stimulates changes in the work culture. Learning in an organization is largely managed internally through periodical skill development programs and experience sharing. The external resources including participatory learning, industrial visits to know best practices, and social interactions to acquire stakeholder and customer perspectives also help employees in an organization to stay updated. Continuous leaning is a process to develop contemporary work culture and information diffusion in an organization.

Culture is a broad term and is often complex in the context of workplace environment or practices. The learning culture delivers many organizational outcomes such as job satisfaction, motivation for learning, and self-actualization over time. However, creating a learning culture in an organization requires behavioral changes among the employees and stakeholders, project its strategic impact. However, there is no unifying definition or theory of learning culture, as it is an agglomeration of several common linear philosophies of quadruple facets comprising knowing, learning, doing, and being. These factors establish the learning culture among the employees and stakeholders in an organization and focus on the following objectives:

- Supporting individual learning
- Motivating creative transformation
- Allowing acquired and learned knowledge to practice
- Developing experience-based strategy and processes
- Encouraging teams to learn and reflect on their work system
- Building proactive influence toward change management
- Driving organization performance to improve through the best practices
- Supporting key organizational decisions

To create a learning-based culture the organizations need to invest in skill development, remove nonprofit barriers, and institute the reward system which facilitate voluntary learning and knowledge enhancement behavior among the employees and stakeholders. The organizational learning culture helps employees in risk-taking, action learning, conducting feedback analysis, and making strategic decisions. In most organizations, human resources look after the effectiveness of the skill development programs in an organization. In collaboration with professional training institutions, inclusive business companies develop learning resources through own programs and explore change management opportunities. New knowledge in these organizations becomes a part of planning and staff training, and is practiced holistically within the organization, which helps them in developing a leadership plan with vision, values, and goals. The knowledge management and continuous learning also help in developing delegation plan with specific task management approach. A priority-based management plan explaining the schedule of tasks, target, and time in combination with the periodic vigilance plan categorically focusing on the monitoring, evaluation, and accountability also emerges as an outcome of the learning and knowledge management process. The organizational learning and collective culture process also educate board members, staff, and stakeholders to work together for a common purpose and build organizational capabilities and competence. Developing learning culture in an organization is an effective way to nurture creativity, architect disrupting patterns of innovation by engaging the stakeholders, and helping the organization to stay competitive in the marketplace.

Continuous learning through updating contemporary information is an essential approach to stay competitive in the changing marketplace. Therefore, organizational learning is a dynamic, multilevel, and nonlinear type of learning in an inclusive organization, which involves both employees and stakeholders. The inclusivity in business develops creative dynamism and analytical skills in learning, while the collective cognition attributes multilevel organizational development (Canbaloğlu et al. 2020). Organizational learning is carried out as the responsibility of effective human resource management and is based on the individual and collective learning of members in an organization. In turn, the capacity of the whole organization to stimulate learning and to generate new knowledge is influenced by the periodical skill development training to reorient employees and stakeholders. Consequently, organizational learning focuses on the work improvement and work management processes and stays as learning organization with continuously changing the work culture and organizational behavior by embedding new learning processes. Learning orientation also embodies vision, mental models, and the cultural factors of organization, which defines a set of organizational values and influences the proactive learning among employees, leaders, and stakeholders (Patky 2020). The organizational improvement and development fundamentally revolve around the general idea of organizational learning. "Solving a problem, introducing a product, and reengineering a process, all require continuous learning by overcoming the old practices and adapting to a new organizational ecosystem" (Garvin 1993).

Many organizations are turning as learning organizations today as business ecosystems are rapidly changing due to the growing political, economic, social, technological, environmental, and legal complexities. Consequently, the business organizations rely heavily on access to high-quality skilled labor. As skilled and well-informed workforce contributes significantly to the organizational performance, recruiting, developing, and retaining the right skills have become the major challenge to the companies. To remain abreast with the changing market dynamics, organizations must think strategically toward investing in human capital and developing the knowledge, skills, and abilities of the workforce. Many organizations tend to upskill or reskill staff quickly, owing to redeployment or to adapt to the hybrid organizational culture combining online to offline transition of work. The ability to learn, adapt, and continuously improve such organization culture has been a major challenge during COVID-19 pandemic paradigm shift. In the skills and learning space, the rising role of platforms driven by technology and automation has emerged as a key driver of contemporary times. Upskilling employees to make effective use of new technologies and developing new knowledge-based sectors such as financial services, sustainability, and pharmaceuticals, upskilling employees has evidenced a more cost-effective strategy. Consequently, companies are investing in training and learning, and recognizing this imperative to stay competitive in the market. Accordingly, the mainstream businesses such as consumer products, health, automobiles, consumer electronics, and green portfolio are engaged in harnessing individual knowledge and learning to continually improve business processes and employee skills. The corporate experience and management studies conducted by human resource consultants indicate that agile strategies, workplace autonomy, and accountability have declined in vulnerable business sectors like industrial products manufacturing and services. Such downward trend revealed that employees need better organization for learning and practicing business improvements. Formal and informal learning is the key for organizations to adapt, and organizations need to ensure continuous learning prospects. The attributes of continuous learning and organizational culture are illustrated in Figure 4.1.

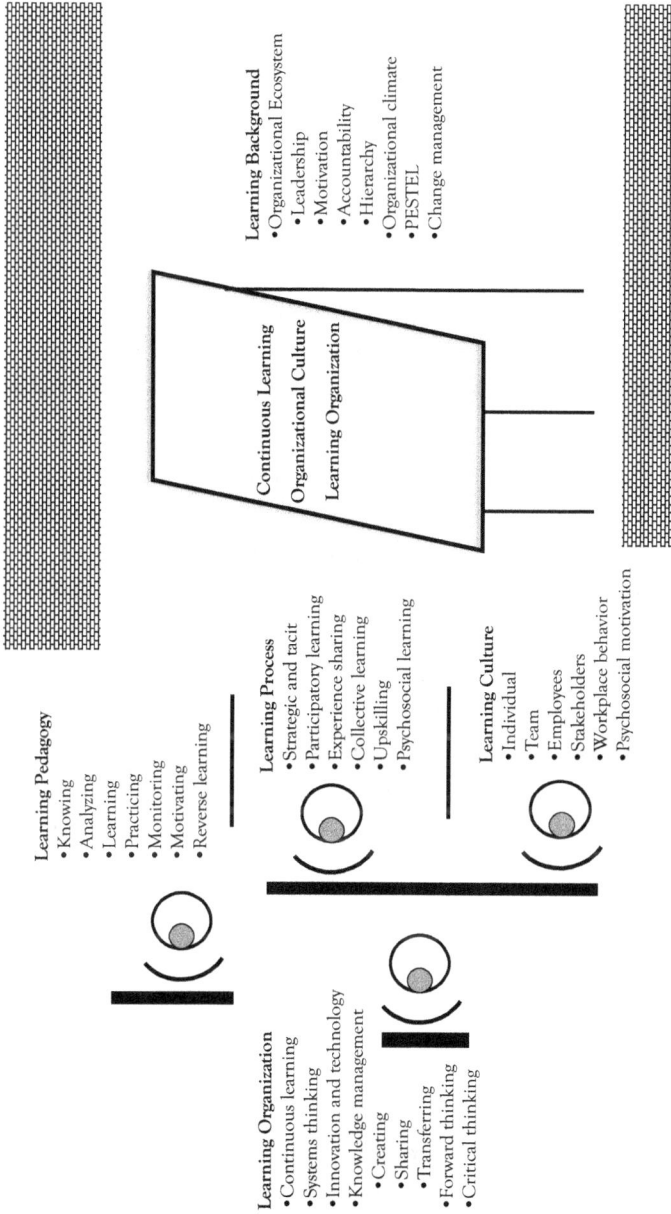

Learning Background
- Organizational Ecosystem
  - Leadership
  - Motivation
  - Accountability
  - Hierarchy
- Organizational climate
- PESTEL
- Change management

Learning Pedagogy
- Knowing
- Analyzing
- Learning
- Practicing
- Monitoring
- Motivating
- Reverse learning

Learning Process
- Strategic and tacit
- Participatory learning
- Experience sharing
- Collective learning
- Upskilling
- Psychosocial learning

Learning Culture
- Individual
- Team
- Employees
- Stakeholders
- Workplace behavior
- Psychosocial motivation

Learning Organization
- Continuous learning
- Systems thinking
- Innovation and technology
- Knowledge management
- Creating
- Sharing
- Transferring
- Forward thinking
- Critical thinking

Continuous Learning
Organizational Culture
Learning Organization

Figure 4.1 Continuous learning and organizational culture

Source: Author

The organizational ecosystem comprising leadership, employee motivation toward continuous learning, accountability, and hierarchy broadly forms the learning background as exhibited in Figure 4.1. In addition, organizational climate and external factors including political, economic, social, technological, environmental, and legal attributes also affect the organizational learning goals and philosophy. Besides, continuous learning in an organization widely depends on the acceptance of employees to the change management, as employee learning and adaptability to new knowledge has a direct relationship with the readiness and nonresistance to the change management in an organization. The continuous learning and organizational culture contribute toward building learning organizations. The continuous learning has four principal domains, which include learning pedagogy, learning process, learning culture, and features of learning organization as presented in Figure 4.1. The learning pedagogy encompasses knowing contemporary practices, analyzing acquired information, learning through outcomes, and practicing and monitoring the knowledge-driven experiments. In addition, the reverse learning has also gained popularity in many companies after being successfully implemented in the GE Company. The reverse learning is a bottom-up learning process, which encourages interactions of junior employees with the higher order executive offering opportunity to share their experience at the bottom of the pyramid. The learning process embeds strategic and tacit knowledge management, participatory learning, experience sharing, collective learning through crowdsourcing, upskilling (advanced training programs), and interactive psychosocial learning. The learning culture in an organization is spread across individuals, teams, employees, and stakeholders, which significantly contribute to the workplace behavior. In view of the earlier discussion, it can be stated that the learning organizations encourage systems thinking, innovative behavior, and broad ways to manage knowledge through creating, sharing, transferring, forward thinking, and critical thinking.

The learning culture embeds learning the process of carrying out tasks by individual employees and team at an organizational level. In building learning culture in an organization, leaders should develop transformation design and develop a strategic model for learning to support employees toward a collectively shared vision and positive change through open dialogue and reflection. The learning environment allows workplaces to integrate psychosocial factors to develop tangible impact on the behaviors of employees and stakeholders to drive dramatic cultural change within the organization. Though there is a large theoretical evidence base on learning culture, the less robust research demonstrates its impact on organizational outcomes in practice. Consequently, the organizational culture is one of the key factors in affecting the success of business. Organizational learning helps in understanding workplace environment and influencing employees and stakeholders at work. However, replicating best practices to improve the organizational system often deters the change management process and fragments the workplace. The organizational culture has shared characteristics among people within the same organization, which include values, behavioral norms, and behavioral perspectives. The organizational climate, on the other hand, surrounds the work setting and the cognitive ergonomics comprising perceptions, emotions, and feelings. These are two concepts that are linked and influence each other, which helps to explain why they are often mistakenly used interchangeably. The learning organizations facilitate continuous transformation in business through adaptation to the changing organizational ecosystem and developing a social approach to organizational performance (Senge 1992). The aim of continuous learning is to enhance organizational capability, tacit knowledge, and experiential learning in the workplace. Theoretically, learning organizations are built with the focus on:

- Supporting individual, collective, and team learning to disseminate knowledge for reshaping the strategies and processes in an organization to improve its performance;
- Influencing employees to acquire and update the knowledge, meet changing business challenges, and cooperate in the transformational process of an organization;
- Teams and the organization are engaged holistically in adapting systems thinking and processes for double-loop learning where individual and group reflections proactively influence changes in an organization;

- Trust, willingness to learn, improve, and change from the
  conventional to contemporary business philosophy are key
  to change management and alternative decision making.
  Consequently, the learning culture is conceptually similar
  to the systems thinking in a learning organization.

Continuous improvement programs through the change management, which involves continuous learning, are multiplying as companies
aim to gain competitive edge. However, the rate of success in this process
remains low due to resistance of the employees and stakeholders to proceed with the change management. To drive a pro-change management
behavior among the employees, the collective decision on learning and
adapting to changes needs to be encouraged (Garvin 1993). To encourage
continuous learning and change management, firms need emphasize on
4Ms comprising motivation, method (process), management, and measurement. The supportive learning environment for continuous learning
comprises psychosocial motivation, appreciation of change with purpose,
openness to new ideas, and extended time for feedback. The sustainable
learning processes and practices include experimentation, information
collection and analysis, and education and training. These elements
can be built as building block for continuous organizational learning
wherein leadership reinforces both learning and change management
(Garvin et al. 2008). Continuous learning in an organization has various
implications. Some of them are stated below:

- Encouraging organizational growth through greater innovation and employee motivation;
- Improving profitability through improved employee performance and stakeholder satisfaction;
- Leading to transformation by a greater capacity to solve problems and respond quickly to changing business conditions; and
- Enhancing productivity in organization at both ends of
  on-the-job productivity and improved talent management.

To motivate the employees, organizations should reward their engagement in continuous learning. The rewarding curiosity not only attracts

praising and drives promoting those who display an effort to learn and develop but also helps in creating a climate that nurtures critical thinking and semantics (Chamorro-Premuzic and Bersin 2018).

Organizational processes and administrative hierarchy often restrict information-sharing and social learning, which affects organizational performance. In addition, "microcultures" within functions and locations build learning attitudes and practices, which vary across organizations by their size and operations. Creating a consistent vision for learning in multilayered and multidomestic organizations is likely to be challenging as the perception toward knowledge management and changing the organizational work culture varies discretely. Teams play a key role in social learning and toward encouraging employees for continuous learning. Managers play a pivotal role and can be more influential for individual learning than developing an overall learning culture in an organization (CIPD 2020). A strong leadership can build a learning culture, which generates transparency in organizational culture and motivates employees to report and analyze in-depth all large and small issues that occur during the organizational learning and change management process. Learning in such transparent culture is proactively sought by the employees and stakeholders. Continuous learning also helps inclusive businesses to explore opportunities, experiment new ideas, and analyze the feedback-loop of customers and stakeholders (Edmondson 2011).

Organizational Learning and Design Thinking

The contemporary trend of collective intelligence meets the challenge of satisfying the growing need for creativity and innovation through brainstorming, especially in product designing and prospective product ergonomics contexts such as space saver products, small automobiles, and multiutility products. The wisdom of crowd helps designers and ergonomists come up with products through crowd-consensus to make appropriate decisions. Promoting creativity through brainstorming is becoming more challenging for firms with increasing knowledge on technology, market competition, and disruptive business trends. Therefore, creativity needs to be fostered through the combined efforts of society and business firms to produce an agile creative workforce to tackle complex tasks (Miller and Dumford 2014). The strategy orientation would drive the brainstorming discussion to result orientation, and the measurability would count on the success of the deliberations. Rapidly changing work culture and complexities of organizational problems demand a quick and judicious managerial decision to drive toward a win-win situation. Fast-cycle decision making is not just about making decisions more quickly. It is a rethinking of the decision-making model where managerial intuition is combined with employees performing brainstorming discussions, carrying out task simulations, and sharing information among the peers. Experiences of project managers drawn from several companies and the leading management studies suggest that the managers' ability to act quickly and wisely depends on his or her personality traits, problem-solving abilities, and managerial relations with the employees (Prewitt 1998). In the progressing companies with the practices of bottom-up decision making and relying on crowd wisdom, brainstorming has been a key tool to generate ideas. The brainstorming exercise is often configured around the following norms (Paulus and Brown 2003):

- Liberal thinking
- Refraining from interpersonal criticism
- Compressive documentation of all the things that come to mind
- Unrestricted steering of contextual ideas
- Generate multistream and multiutility ideas
- Pooling of ideas and later screening with quality indicators
- Encouraging development of intertwined and relevant ideas.

Openly and actively communicating with employees, for example, earns their trust and engagement. To develop participation in the developing innovation project plan and budgeting, project managers should go beyond brainstorming among the stakeholders and sponsor. The project team should link strategy and purpose with project and initiative development by implementing a process of idea generation, selection, and conversion, known as *front-end innovation*. Once the project charter is complete, the debate on project budgeting can be initiated by assessing the adequacy of financial resources, people, and competencies to execute innovation plans. The project team can accordingly make changes in hiring people, cost estimations, and contingency planning with required skills (Joan and Joaquim 2015). As discussed earlier, the wisdom of crowd leading to collective intelligence can be broadly networked with three process factors comprising brainstorming, semantics, and design thinking.

In large organizations, design perspectives are becoming central to the process of business modeling and strategy implementation. The concept of business design has emerged over time as a collective approach in an organization involving customers, stakeholders, and key functional partners. Most organizations have realized today that staying in business as learning organizations helps them grow competitively and consistently in the marketplace. Such business maxim has been described as "systems thinking" that leads to the design principle in business, known as "design thinking." Companies pursue this concept as a response to the mounting complexities in business operations. Design thinking in business has been conceived as an essential tool for simplifying the business operation by interlinking organization, society, and stakeholders, and more comprehensively humanizing the business. The extended principles of design thinking in business converge with the market attributes (market players, ethics, and business growth), social responsiveness (marketing with purpose), and customers' (stakeholders') value propositions.

Consumer behavior is growing complex with the advancement of frugal and disruptive innovations, and affordable technologies such as social, domestic, and light industrial robots that influence customers. The rapid and abrupt shifts in consumer behavior have thrown major challenges of achieving market competitiveness and consistent lead to the customer-centric companies. Therefore, the design thinking has become a popular tool to develop customer-centric marketing strategies. The design-to-market strategies have helped companies cocreate products for customers with high perceived use value. IKEA home décor, furniture, and fixtures based on the need and design suggested by the customers; Lego Creation from static models to power driven creations; and simplified Oral-B electric toothbrush from P&G which has reduced from many functions to two for customer convenience set the right examples of the use of design thinking to induce consumer behavior. Conventionally, design has been a downstream perspective in the product development process for the high-value customer segment. Over time, with the convergence of collective intelligence and customer research, firms have focused on developing new products with perceived aesthetics and inculcating brand perception among customers. The digital and reminiscent advertising of products have helped firms in making customers understand about the design attributes in products and perceive values. Consequently, the design thinking has gone public today and is known for its contributions in marketing with customers. The design and innovation encompass collective intelligence that exhibits not only the customer demand but also the emotions associated with the products and buying decisions. The emotions and personality of customers associated with the products are evolved around the creative ideas, product attributes, complementarity, and user-oriented designs. These factors significantly contribute to the design-to-market concepts of developing and managing new products rather than simply managing them with a conventional marketing strategy. Design thinking has been emerged as a method to deliver needs and desires of customers through streamlined solutions, which could attain high market share. The design process is carried out in a technologically feasible and strategically viable (cost-time-risk-profit) manner. The most challenging situation in the design thinking process is the radical change in cost-time-risk factors combined with customer brainstorming and rapid prototyping. Most design-to-market products are developed using innovative processes and software that radically streamline information exchange between the companies, stakeholders, and key partners (Brown 2008).

As customer preferences are changing rapidly, companies developing design thinking in the strategies consider the competitive leverage over the time. Companies tend to reach customers and offer them competitive benefits through cocreated organizational practices and design. Shifts in the market processes in the society are induced by fundamental beliefs and shared assumptions and resemble elements of social culture defining norms of markets, expected behavior, and thought. Most firms know their customers sketchily, and the marketing strategies are based on their innate assumption, competitive response, and rapid guesswork than scientific analysis of customer insights and strategic requirements. The rapid and abrupt shifts in consumer behavior have thrown major

challenges to the customer-centric companies to achieve market competitiveness and consistent lead. The elements of marketing-mix have
evolved over the years in reference to the changing business environment,
shifts in industry focus, and government regulations. Customer-centric
businesses derive in-depth insights into what, how, and with whom
customers want to interact during the cocreation process. Advances in
digital technologies have augmented the scope of outsourcing business
activities beyond geographic boundaries through several independent
contributors. The collective insights develop cocreated business models
to drive an impact in emerging market through popular attributes of
products, pricing, promotions, packaging, and managing customer psychodynamics based on collectively generated contents. Innovation of new
products is a complex process that needs to be carried out meticulously in
the firms integrating the business and customer use values in the marketplace. The interrelationship between organizational learning and design
thinking is presented in Figure 4.2.

The organizational learning and design thinking is an agile process,
which is founded on the liberal social environment at the workplace.
The design thinking is evolved on the four distinctive elements of design
thinking, design thinking process, and the iterative working practice in an
organization as exhibited in Figure 4.2. The design thinking philosophy
is based on the human-centered approach to innovation by integrating
people, technology, and business. The designer's toolkit serves as the key
driver in the designing thinking practice. The 4-D design factors include
the challenge to discover the right perspectives considering the problems,
needs, and desired solutions (PNS factors) required by the users. The PNS
factors can be discovered by perceptual mapping of users and through the
semantics (interrelated thoughts). The design can be developed through
the collaboration of stakeholders, crowd anchors, or public–private partnership. A major challenge in design thinking is the delivery of design output. To strengthen the design delivery, it is necessary for the organization
to develop market segmentation, targeting, and positioning strategies.
The process of design thinking is exhibited in Figure 4.2, which reveals
that it moves though the five principal stages including discovering the
design goals through crowdsourcing and collective intelligence. The stage
is followed by defining the innovative design objective and developing

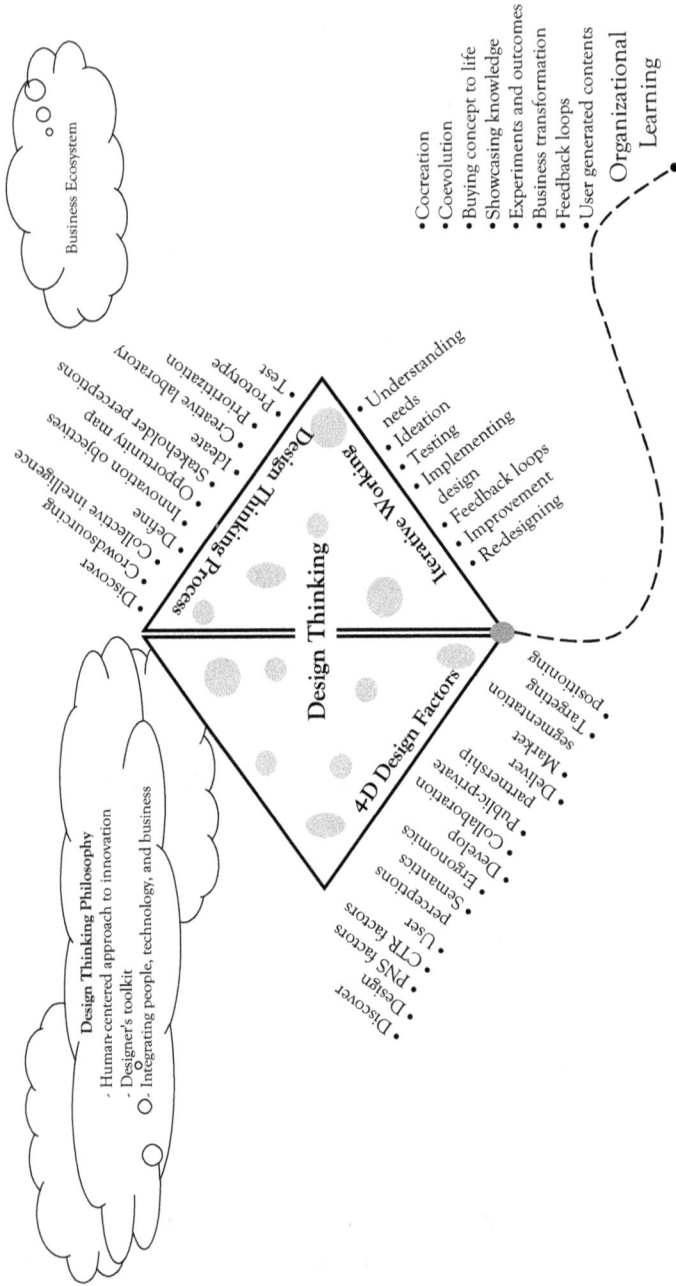

Figure 4.2 Organizational learning and design thinking

Source: Author

opportunity map based on the perceptions of stakeholders and users. Properly discovering and defining the needs and objectives of user-centric designing, organizations are set for ideation on design through creative laboratories (institutional, social, and crowd-based platforms), and prioritize the design process. Accordingly, prototype is designed and tested prior to its commercialization. The design thinking is an iterative process and looped until the output is finalized for delivery. The design thinking is continuously evolved in a loop through continuous ideation, testing, implementation, analyzing the feedback loops, and considering improvement and redesigning. Effective learning organizations support design thinking, cocreation, coevolution, and experimenting various outcome of learning. In addition, learning organizations tend to showcase knowledge to help employees and stakeholders in business transformation process through feedback loops and user-generated contents.

In large organizations, design thinking is becoming central to enterprise performance and a key indicator in achieving market competitiveness (e.g., Hoogveld 2017). Such design orientation intensively supports the marketing strategy of firms than holding merely the aesthetics values and product development process. Crowdsourcing design ideas is an emerging process of design thinking throughout the organization. The crowd design approach is time-taking and piles up information in an unclassified bin unless carefully segments on digital platforms. The crowd design ideas deal with huge responses and meet the complex challenges for many products, services, and processes. However, crowd design projects need programmed interactions with technologies and other complicated systems as a design project and stimulate the participants to be intuitive and pleasurable. Therefore, design thinking is an essential tool for simplifying and humanizing the collective ideas for crowd (mass customers). The principles of crowd-based design thinking include many attributes, some are listed below:

- Focus on customer experiences
- Exploring emotions
- Creation of physical models, such as diagrams and sketches
- Manifesting ideas to resolve social or consumption problems

- Use of prototypes to experiment with solutions
- Critical success factors, expected problems, and a tolerance for failure
- Limiting product features to avoid complexities and ensure ease of use of technology.

Creating a design-centric culture involving crowd requires continuous motivation to promote quality designs so that the returns on investment in design can be ensured, though it is difficult to measure (Kolko 2015).

The crowd-based design thinking has become popular in many customer-centric firms, and this practice has been pioneered by IKEA, Samsung, and Harley Davidson. These firms have tried to explore customer perceptions through crowd-based designing and evoke designers' problem-solving techniques to innovate products. Key elements of the design thinking methodology include exploring and applying user-generated contents, carrying our early and frequent interaction with customers, developing agile process design, and the learning-by-doing approach. The crowd-designing process involves sharing ideas, building prototypes, and creating mock-ups of any kind at the quickest possible time to launch in the market. The design thinking initiatives have been frequently floated though the social media by the start-up companies, and such initiatives rarely proceed according to a prescribed business model. Such crowd initiatives are focused on agile and frugal innovation concepts, which are initially aimed at a niche market. Crowd-based innovation is initially an unfiltered process with hidden conflicts and complications on design processes and structures. The raw data on crowd design might not be congruent with the corporate objectives and cultures. Therefore, firms critically analyze the crowd-design data and measure the cost, time, and risk factors in adapting to the ideas from the crowd information pool. The design thinking methodology encourages democratic and self-organized teams. However, most large companies work with the hierarchical decision-making process. In fact, the design thinking teams work for outsourced ideation process with the clear project charter defining processes and the expected outcome. Such projects are managed by senior managers who constitute small crowd groups and supervise design thinking projects on spatial and temporal dimensions (Kupp et al. 2017). The design-thinking process embeds following steps:

- Effective coordination between managers and users (crowd groups) in managing design thinking initiatives;
- Developing balance between emotions, intuitions, and analytical thinking among design thinking teams;
- Establishing ground rules to systematically draft the design process;
- Providing adequate autonomy to the design thinking teams to operate with liberal cognitive space integrating design thinking process into the product development processes;
- Encouraging design thinking as a continuous learning project rather than an isolated exercise; and
- Measuring profits as the metrics for design thinking projects upon commercializing the designs.

In large organizations, design perspectives are becoming central to the process of business modeling and strategy implementation. The concept of business design has emerged over time as a collective approach in an organization involving customers, stakeholders, and key functional partners. Most organizations have realized today that staying in business as learning organizations helps them grow competitively and consistently in the marketplace. Such business maxim has been described as "systems thinking" that leads to the design principle in business, known as "design thinking." Companies pursue this concept as a response to the mounting complexities in business operations. Design thinking in business has been conceived as an essential tool for simplifying the business operation by interlinking organization, society, and stakeholders, and more comprehensively humanizing the business. The extended principles of design thinking in business converge with the market attributes (market players, ethics, and business growth), social responsiveness (marketing with purpose), and customers' (stakeholders') value propositions. Design thinking has been emerged as a method to deliver needs and desires of customers through streamlined solutions, which could attain high market share. The design process is carried out in a technologically feasible and strategically viable (cost–time–risk–profit) manner. The most challenging situation in the design thinking process is the radical change in cost–time–risk factors combined with customer brainstorming and rapid prototyping (Rajagopal 2021).

Most organizations manage individual design teams through the initials stage of idea generation to its commercialization process. In this process, it is important to establish clear rationale and objectives, choose right design-thinking methods, and integrate key partners and resources to market the designed product. The aforementioned stages are sensitive touch points in the design thinking and outsourcing of design activities. One of the critical requirements for the crowd-based design projects is communicating clear directions on the process and simultaneously managing the cost, time, and risk factors associated with the design process. However, incremental prototyping and testing of design is an internal marketing project helps in measuring the success and failure of designs by markets and customer segments. Consequently, firms need to manage the design processes in both internal and external ecosystem. Employees, market players, and stakeholders need to be provided with continuous guidance and support from corporate and social leaders to manage product designs competitive and profitable. In crowd-based designing process, though the role of crowd-group leaders and investors is primary, the executives of the firm stay on top of such innovation projects and lead them to success. Diverse businesses like PepsiCo and Airbnb have successfully implemented the design thinking process using collective intelligence to launch products and services, respectively. The design thinking is refined over time in many firms and is integrated with stage gate process to implement checks and balances effectively in the design process. The stage gate process is an integrated part of project management and is used today to create innovations. Many firms today have installed the Stage-Gate innovation system which is a process of phased project reviews to develop new products and services (Nakata 2020).

The rapid and abrupt shifts in consumer behavior have thrown major challenges of achieving market competitiveness and consistent lead to the customer-centric companies. Therefore, design thinking has become a popular tool to develop customer-centric marketing strategies. The design-to-market strategies have helped companies cocreate products for customers with high perceived use value. IKEA home décor, furniture, and fixtures based on the need and design suggested by the customers; Lego Creation from static models to power-driven creations; and simplified Oral-B electric toothbrush from P&G, which has reduced from many functions to two for customer convenience set the right examples of the use of design thinking to induce consumer behavior. Conventionally, design has been a downstream perspective in the product development process for the high-value customer segment. Over time, with the convergence of collective intelligence and customer research, firms have focused on developing new products with perceived aesthetics and inculcating brand perception among customers. The digital and reminiscent advertising of products have helped firms in making customers understand about the design attributes in products and perceive values. Consequently, the design thinking has gone public today and is known for its contributions in marketing with customers. Successful companies like Nestlé, Whole Foods, and Apple bring business and society back together by creating shared value and generating economic value, using collective intelligence. Companies deliver value through collective designing of social products for society by addressing its challenges.

Wearable products like the Nike *FuelBand* are transforming the idea of branded activity through social consciousness. The *FuelBand* allows customers to set goals, track progress, and celebrate achievements. The information from the wristband is then integrated into existing online networks like Facebook. Simply by wearing the band, consumers' fitness activity is now branded "Nike." This is an example of convergence of social and commercial products designed through collective intelligence. As digital sharing is becoming a part of our daily experience, the brands will benefit most through socially conscious lifestyle. The social and value-oriented business designs tend to reconceive products and markets based on the social needs, redefine productivity in the value chain, and build social innovation clusters at their business hubs. Social collaborations focus on improving both business processes and performance. Social orientation of a business starts from a niche, links corporate-interest to shared interest, encourages productive competition, cocreates values, and builds trust among customers.

Systems Thinking

Systems thinking as an idea can be applied in various scientific fields including planning and evaluation, education, business and management, public health, sociology and psychology, cognitive science, human development, agriculture, sustainability, environmental sciences, ecology and biology, earth sciences, and other physical sciences. Systems thinking can influence many of the existing concepts, theories, and knowledge in each of these fields (Cabrera et al. 2008). In marketing and related business strategies, managers need to think ahead of the competitors to keep moving from niche to market leader status. However, systems thinking does reframe how we think about what we view as a problem in the first place, and what solutions might look like. The reasons for the scientific utility and promise of systems thinking are extensive. Systems thinking and agility in business are complimentary as continuous learning and knowledge management drive both the ability of reasoning and agility (Cegarra-Navarro et al. 2016). The agility in businesses includes workplace culture, decision making, operations, technology, innovation, and customer behavior at the bottom-line comprising people, profit, and sustainability. Understanding people is connected to the personality, social values, and ethnicity. Advances in digital technologies have increased the possibilities of developing agile business models by outsourcing business activities to crowds comprising contributors. Using the collective intelligence of a crowd opens a new range of knowledge outreach and power of collective reasoning and decision making with agility and conformity (Rajagopal 2022).

Systems thinking in developing marketing strategy is considered as a disciplined approach to promote competitive behavior of firms in a marketplace. To develop systems thinking approach in a business organization requires a substantial change in the organizational culture (O'Connor 1997). This approach would be helpful in resolving the various business conflicts, some of which are listed below:

- Multiple perspectives on a situation causing dilemma over its management;
- Consumer behavior oscillating endlessly;

- A previously applied strategies seeming to overshoot the goal and affect related areas of operation;
- The tendency to stay weak in negotiations over time;
- Problems in establishing procedural standards in the business operations;
- Decline in business growth over time;
- Lack of efforts in developing core competencies; and
- Optimization of resources and their business application for augmenting growth in vital business indicators in the firm.

The systems thinking is usually driven by many smaller systems or subsystems. For example, an organization is made up of many administrative and management functions, products, services, groups, and individuals. If one part of the system is changed, the nature of the overall system is often changed as well by definition. Systems theory has brought a new perspective for managers to interpret patterns and events in their organizations. Effective systems methodology lies at the intersection of the following four foundations of systems thinking (Ackoff 1999; Gharajedaghi 2006):

- Holistic thinking focuses on the systems logic and process orientation in general. Reviewing the system in totality requires understanding structure, function, process, and context at the same time. The systems approach enables connecting objects of various types to a single platform of thinking to organize different forms of activity within the given time and space of the situation in business. One of the principal requirements of each successful system is an effective communication among different actions. The effective development of the organization can be achieved when various strategies, strategic planning, teamwork, and principles of organizational changes are applied. Technical aspects are combined with the aspects of behavior, personal (personal mastery and intellectual models) with conceptual ones.
- Operational thinking, which also signifies dynamic thinking, refers to the conception of the principles of systems dynamics, that is, evaluation of the multiloop feedback systems, identi-

fication of the delay effect and barriers of growth, mapping stock and flow, and so on. The conception of these principles creates an additional value for managing organization in reference to business systems that emerge as an interdependent factor in decision making (Skarzauskiene 2010).

- Interactivity is a design of the desirable future and a search for its implementation ways. Interactive design is both the art of finding differences among things that seem similar and the science of finding similarities among things that seem different. The distinct outputs of interactive design may lead to defining problems, identifying the leverage point, and designing solutions-ideation process.

- Interactive design is a part of critical thinking that defines a problem, gathering of information for problem solution, formulation of hypotheses, checking presumptions and correctness of findings, making a solution. Interactive design offers a constant critical assessment, continuous learning, and understanding of mental models. This dimension of systems thinking is based on intuitive thinking that stimulates creativity and provides an organization with a conceptual foundation to create a unique competitive advantage.

In view of the fast-growing market competition, more and more companies are recognizing the business opportunities created by a focus on sustainability. Such a shift in thinking in many companies and industries, where learning organization principles are being applied to create sustainable business models, has evidenced changes in organizational culture and improvement in the core competencies. Simultaneously, they become inspirational, energetic places to work where even relationships with customers and suppliers improve. However, a more integrated view can enable companies to innovate for long-term profitability and sustainability. There are three core competencies that learning organizations must master to profit from sustainability include encouraging systemic thinking and convene strategic market players and customers toward changing conventional thinking and take the lead in reshaping economic, political, and societal forces that baffle change (Senge and Carstedt 2001).

Crowd-based information offers a powerful metaphor that inspires diverse strategic frameworks to develop services business modeling in cocreating customer experiences and values. Collective intelligence helps firms extend the outreach of services within communities. Consumer journey frameworks offer a crowd-based approach to explore customer experience and provide structured services for managing experiences by emphasizing how to improve touchpoints strategically (Lemon and Verhoef 2016). Technological advances have fostered the Internet of Things vision, in which systems are inherently cyber-physical, increasingly contextual, and opportunistic in nature. On the information infrastructure side, Cloud, Fog, and Edge Computing provide virtualized services to manage collective intelligence. The mosaics of collective intelligence on services can be mapped over time and space to develop semantics of services management, which induces complex interdependencies between idea generation and collective management of services (Martel et al. 2017).

In large organizations, design perspectives are becoming central to the process of business modeling and strategy implementation. The concept of business-design has emerged over time as a collective approach in an organization involving customers, stakeholders, and key functional partners. Most organizations have realized today that staying in business as learning organizations helps them grow competitively and consistently in the marketplace. Such business maxim has been described as "systems thinking" that leads to the design principle in business, known as "design thinking." Companies pursue this concept as a response to the mounting complexities in business operations. Design thinking in business has been conceived as an essential tool for simplifying the business operation by interlinking organization, society, and stakeholders, and more comprehensively humanizing the business involving crowd in innovation and ideation process. The extended principles of design thinking in business converge with the market attributes (market players, ethics, and business growth), social responsiveness (marketing with purpose), and customers' (stakeholders') value propositions. Design thinking has been emerged as a method of delivering needs and desires of customers through streamlined solutions, which could attain high market share. The design process is carried out in a technologically feasible and strategically viable (cost–time–risk–profit) manner. The most challenging situation in the design thinking process is the radical change in cost–time–risk factors combined with customer brainstorming and rapid prototyping (Rajagopal 2021).

Developing systems thinking and planned layout of business strategies by firms to enhance growth and competitiveness drive managerial symphony. Firms offer a variety of tactical strategies to achieve business growth in a short time and measuring economic and social risk. However, companies with long-term vision develop cross-cultural marketing expertise through building brand image, competitive management, sharing and analyzing market information, and developing intimacy with customers to lead in the market (Rajagopal 2012). Organizing and planning management ideas in a schematic manner leads to systems thinking, and is said to hold great promise. The systems approach, which is also synonymous to managerial symphony, is viewed as taxonomy to gain sustainable growth in the competitive marketplace. For a manager to become a systems thinker and symphony organizer, he or she needs to spend years learning competitive strategies and apply them appropriately to witness transformative results (Cabrera et al. 2008).

Systems consist of people, structures, technologies, and processes that work together to make organizations viable. Systems thinking, a part of operations and management research, essentially looks at the whole as a basis for understanding, designing, and managing its components. Systems thinking is applied in organizational management for decades in the field of operations, but it has also been conceptualized in the functional areas of marketing. Systems thinking offers a powerful new perspective, a synchronized flow of thoughts, and a set of tools that can be used to address the most complex problems in everyday business operations. Systems thinking may be considered as a way of understanding reality that emphasizes the relationships among various components in a process, rather than the independent constituents of the process. Based on the attitude of the employees toward change proneness, the systems thinking in innovation works effectively with proactive strategies of the company. Accordingly, the company can harness creative potential while maintaining accountability instead of reacting to employees for resisting to change. Most organizations clarify the roles of each employee in the innovation process while enhancing organizational flexibility, aligning internal processes to facilitate change and build the innovation leadership pipeline in association with the customers and stakeholders (Judge 2011).

Based on a field of study known as system dynamics, systems thinking has a practical value that rests on a solid theoretical foundation. In marketing operations, systems thinking can be described as a tool in tracing and linking various activities in a particular function. To be competitive, companies must develop innovative new businesses on competitive market platforms. Firms may face several operational barriers and seldom mesh smoothly with well-established systems, processes, and cultures. Nonetheless, success requires a balance of conventional and new marketing strategies to keep the competitive forces in equilibrium (Garvin and Levesque 2006). Emerging companies face various challenges when they pursue new businesses and the usual problematic responses to those challenges. The systems thinking is usually driven by many smaller systems or subsystems. For example, an organization is made up of many administrative and management functions, products, services, groups, and individuals. If one part of the system is changed, the nature of the overall system also changes by definition. Systems theory has brought a new perspective for managers to interpret the patterns and events in their organizations. Organizational system consists of people (crowd), structures (policies), technologies (infrastructure), and processes (manufacturing and marketing) that work together to make organizations viable. Of these elements of the system, crowdsourcing has emerged as one of the strongest approaches for customer-centric cocreation and coevolution of innovation projects. Systems thinking therefore has emerged today as a part of collective research, which essentially looks at the whole as a basis for understanding, designing, and managing its component parts (Norton 2010).

Interactive design offers a constant critical assessment, and continuous learning and understanding of mental models. This dimension of systems thinking is based on intuitive thinking that stimulates creativity and provides an organization with a conceptual foundation to create a unique competitive advantage. The success of systems thinking approach needs a transformational leadership at both business organizations to help in redesigning organization, creating value chain, developing global standards, investing in business process improvement, and strengthening the backward and forward business linkages. The business growth lies in building synergy between the society and the business firms. The concept of synergy refers to the achievement by integrating the social values with business goals for developing competitiveness, trust among consumers, and ensuring growth. The concept drives the firms to make an additional effort over the sum of the conventional decisions focused on market leadership and profit-oriented business goals. Systems thinking stimulates cooperation between several elements, and allows for greater overall effects integrating the social and business values (Carayannis and Campbell 2009). The coevolution of small and big companies enhances investment on innovation, technology, and research and development. Such mergers or acquisitions help companies strengthen their marketing strategies by developing customer-centric branding and promotion strategies. The convergence of technology, entrepreneurship education, and public policies on entrepreneurship development programs promote hybridization, business performance, and corporate citizenship behavior ambidextrously between small and large enterprises.

It is observed that knowledge management fully mediates the impact of organizational culture on organizational effectiveness, and partially mediates the impact of organizational structure and strategy on organizational effectiveness. There is a possible mediating role of knowledge management in managing relationship between the systems thinking attributes comprising organizational goals, employee engagement, stakeholder values, work culture, decision-making process, and organizational effectiveness (Zheng et al. 2010). The systems thinking is usually driven by many smaller systems or subsystems. For example, an organization is made up of many administrative and management functions, products, services, groups, and individuals. If one part of the system is changed, the nature of the overall system also changes by definition. Systems theory has brought a new perspective for managers to interpret the patterns and events in their organizations.

Organizational Mission and Vision

Every organization drafts a clear mission and vision to portray the organizational path, highlighting the current and future priorities to work with. A clear statement of mission and vision engages employees in learning about the work-culture and dynamic growth process of an organization. Clarity of mission and vision statements also educates the stakeholders and business partners about the competitive growth pattern and goals of the organization in the competitive business environment. Mission and vision integrate the principal objectives of an organization and are typically communicated in a simple statement. Mission and vision are statements that offer answers to the questions about the purpose of the organization, stakeholder values, and the workplace culture. Organizations that clearly communicate the mission and vision statements make employees and stakeholders understand the organizational philosophy clearly. The organizational effectiveness can be higher when strategies are perfectly aligned with their goals and objectives. Mission statements are often longer than vision statements. Values associated with the organization are sometimes summarized in mission statements. Organizational values are the beliefs of the employees and stakeholders in which they are emotionally growing (Bart et al. 2001). Mission statements of business organizations commonly focus on the following attributes:

- Workplace environment
- Diversity and integrity
- Relevance and excellence
- Enthusiasm, continuous learning, and innovation
- Positive thinking
- Profitability, growth, and success

Unlike mission statement, a vision statement of an organization focuses on future perspectives and delineates its competitive goals and aspirations. A mission statement lays the organization's current priorities, while the vision statement emphasizes new goals to be achieved over time. The strategy tends to flow directly from the vision to satisfy the organization's mission. The vision statements are typically time-oriented and relatively brief. The mission statement largely depicts the chronological evolutions and the embedded organizational values. However, the vision statement portrays the competitive posture of the organization in the industry. The mission and vision statements guide organizations in developing strategies to reach the set objectives and evaluate performance.

Marketing today is not just a profit phenomenon for most successful global and multidomestic companies; it is rather a ensuring a sustained growth in marketplace by creating social and stakeholder values. Consequently, the business models are built around triadic constituents including market (competition), society (social needs, responsibility, and sustainability), and values (customers and stakeholders). These elements are integrated to explain the design cube through the design-to-market, design-to-society, and design-to-value perspectives in contemporary business modeling process (Rajagopal 2021a). The major concern for large firms today is not to explore new markets, expand portfolios, and go global but to tailor their business strategies to fit to social, ethnic, and consumer culture. Such strategic alignment determines the degree of standardization or adaptation appropriate to the society, stakeholders, and customers in creating strategic. Firms converge the design cube elements and build overall business strategy, determining which products and services benefit in the competitive, social, and consumption ecosystems. Accordingly, companies develop strengths to defy social and cultural barriers and analyze trade-offs to develop appropriate the marketing mix strategies (e.g., Quelch and Hoff 1986).

Some organizations like Intel, Microsoft, Apple, GE, and Cisco have practiced cocreating mission and vision statements for their organization over the years, and they periodically revise engaging employees and stakeholders. The ZOPP (*Zielorientierte Projektplanung* in German) or GOPP (Goal Oriented Project Planning in English) approach is used and promoted by the *Deutsche Gesellschaft für Technische Zusammenarbeit* (GTZ), a German Technical Cooperation, to demonstrate the process of developing collaborative statements of mission either for an organization, or for a specific project. The ZOPP approach provides a systematic structure for identification, planning, and management of projects and tasks in a workshop setting. In this process, employees and stakeholders are asked to delineate the most appropriate goal for their organization, suggest the most suitable approach to achieve the suggested goal, fix accountability to carry out the approach, and identify the potential problems in achieving the set goal. The above information collected from various key employees of the organization is documented and categorized, and the common output is used to develop the draft of mission statement of the organization. Developing such mission and vision statements exhibits employee commitment and adherence to the personal values associated with these statements. Employee and stakeholder collaboration in developing such statements develops emotions, affinity, loyalty, and commitment among them to collectively reach the determined goals in an organization. The ZOPP output generates collaborative matrix on the basis of logical framework, which identifies the key performance indicators, and structures the main elements of an organization or project to achieve goals. This approach highlights logical linkages between intended inputs, planned activities, and expected results. In applied project management context, ZOPP is employed widely by the large donor organizations because of the orderly structuring and documentation of information, and its demand for more skill generation in the project process.

ZOPP requires a moderator with a high degree of experience and skill. The GTZ often engages a highly trained consultant to moderate this exercise, and a special course must be completed to achieve status of a moderator. At the level of an organization, this exercise may take more than a day, depending on the number of areas and employees associated with the company. The ZOPP has two phases: analysis and project planning. The analysis phase has the following four steps, with the identification of "real" problems as the driver for the exercises.

- Participation analysis: This part is related to the presentation of an overview of persons, functional areas, stakeholders, and alliance companies connected to an organization or a specific project. The interests, motives, attitudes, and implications toward the organization growth are documented.
- Point of view (POV) analysis: All POVs are grouped into a problem tree with cause and effect, and identification of the core problem. The problems are documented and organized by smaller groups.
- Objectivity analysis: A restatement of the problems into realistically achievable goals; this is often done by rewriting the problems into outcomes, often by reversing the cards.
- Alternative analysis: Identification of objectives and assessment of alternatives according to resources, probability of achieving objectives, political feasibility, cost–benefit ratio, social risks, time horizon, sustainability, and others factors as decided by the group.

The ZOPP exercise is known for its rigidity and rigor, and it engages all participants to actively share their opinion to construct the mission and vision statements. Quantitative and qualitative performance and impact indicators are defined during the exercise. These indicators provide a simple and reliable means to measure the achievements and results of the set mission and vision of an organization or a specific project.

Case Studies on Leaning Systems

Mukamas: A Learning Agglomerate

The culture of learning reveals in the performance of an organization. However, the pertinent question that raises a big quest is how a culture of learning can be consciously built as a basis for the continuous learning among the individuals, teams, and the community. *Mukamas*, a Finnish learning design company, believes that business activities begin from the individual learning to team learning, which further leads to the collective intelligence. However, a sustainable learning system and framework needs to be integrated as the organizational learning culture. The company facilitates agile, transformational learning processes for large companies, public sector organizations, and development networks. The overall aim of *Mukamas* is to create more agile, learning-based culture as workplaces by developing learning capabilities for teams and individual employees. The company enables business organizations continuously to co-develop learning process with fellow learners, stakeholders, and key partners. Learning is considered today as the digital tool for knowledge management in the form of both synchronous and asynchronous (analyzing and doing) pedagogy. The company embraces the learning philosophy as knowing, analyzing, learning, doing, and being which meets the standards of relevance (knowledge) and excellence (skill development) with the organization.

Mukamas is engaged in supporting people in improving their individual learning skills and journey in contributing to the performance of organization. Therefore, the transformational leadership model and work practices need to support and enable learning in every way. For instance, superiors and team leaders serving as learning coaches help to facilitate continuous experimenting and brainstorming in teams for adopting new ideas and challenges of change management. In addition, *Mukamas* promotes sharing and learning in communities as a cultivated practice. The company is usually connected to an individual's desire or need to develop a subject- or task-related aspect within their organization. Accordingly, the company encourages the individuals to start or join a community of practice, and share knowledge and experiences to intertwine learning and practice ambidextrously.

It has been observed in the company that working as a facilitator and a coach of learning design and leadership in different kinds of development projects need a grassroots approach to support the transition of knowledge to the day-to-day requirements. The trainers of the company build an effective dialogue among all the participants. The interactive platform *Howspace* of the company is a very natural part of the training process with the familiar features from social media. The platform office is a workspace where they can safely share their thoughts and ideas, even with the topic that might be a bit sensitive for different kind of conversations. With a big group of participants, it's important to get everyone involved in some way, reflecting on and discussing the issues. The goal of skill development should be to create an inspirational agenda to kick-off the learning process.

GE Bottom-Up Communication

The GE Company has made two sweeping changes in communication and transparency in the organization, which encouraged employees to resolve common problems together and fearlessly provide constructive feedback. Such practice has made the GE to become one of the foremost learning organizations. In the early 1980s, the organizational culture of the company had strict top-down hierarchy and conventional knowledge silos. The organizational hierarchy can be explained in the two scenarios. In the first scenario, a manager in one division had to read seven reports every day, of which one report is routinely too long, while in another case, the head of a department couldn't sign for approval without a supervisor's approval.

Jack Welch, the CEO of the GE (1981–2001), recognized that his company needed to be transformed as a boundaryless organization and focused on employee engagement and open communication across departments. Consequently, the company had initiated a Work-Out process, which physically brought employees together to share knowledge and resolve common problems collaboratively. Such practice has resulted in an unrestrained flow of expertise, and ideas led to better communication and quicker decisions, contributing to GE's rise to a high-stake company globally. Later, the company introduced the concept and practice of reverse mentoring to help junior employees teach senior executives about the Internet by reversing the organizational practice. It was a wealth of source to learn the applied aspects of the behavior of key partners and stakeholders at the BOP. The benefits of reverse mentoring stand valued even today as it helps in developing relationships with senior leaders lead cross-experience learning to an ease of communication and feedback.

Jack Welch believed that rigid, hierarchical organizations were poorly structured to compete in the fast-moving, information-centric, customer-focused competitive environment, and so on. GE recognized the significance of the diversity of knowledge, talents, and ideas which serves as an effective competitive weapon for the company in the new business environment. Work-Out, GE's boundary-breaking program of the early 1990s, made GE a boundaryless company, and launched boundarylessness both as a management philosophy and a potential field of study. Boundaryless learning and performing experience have grown across quadruple directions comprising vertical, horizontal, external, and geographic dimensions. Among these, the horizontal and vertical dimensions have been most important for the understanding of boundarylessness at GE because those were the two dimensions concerned with day-to-day interactions among co-workers. There are few instances which helped in pointing and pushing strategy in GE. The most notable among them is the training on six sigma given to employees. Learning and practicing the six-sigma approaches by GE employees helped the company in improving quality of its products. At GE, boundaryless behavior was recommended and thrusted upon the employees as a priority toward learning, analyzing, implementing, and monitoring the organizational performance.

References

Ackoff, R.L. 1999. *Ackoff's Best: His Classic Writings on Management*. New York, NY: John Wiley & Sons.

Bart, C.K., N. Bontis, and S. Taggar. 2001. "A Model of the Impact of Mission Statements on Firm Performance." *Management Decision* 39, no. 1, pp. 19–35.

Brown, T. 2008. "Design Thinking." *Harvard Business Review* 86, no. 6, pp. 84–92.

Cabrera, D., L. Colosi, and C. Lobdell. 2008. "Systems Thinking." *Evaluation and Program Planning* 31, no. 3, pp. 299–310.

Canbaloğlu, G., J. Treur, and P.H.M.P. Roelofsma. 2020. "Computational Modeling of Organizational Learning by Self-Modeling Networks." *Cognitive Systems Research* 73, pp. 51–64.

Carayannis, E.G., and D.F. Campbell. 2009. "'Mode 3' and 'Quadruple Helix': Toward a 21st Century Fractal Innovation Ecosystem." *International Journal of Technology and Management* 46, no. 3–4, pp. 201–234.

Cegarra-Navarro, J.G., P. Soto-Acosta, and A.K. Wensley. 2016. "Structured Knowledge Processes and Firm Performance: The Role of Organizational Agility." *Journal of Business Research* 69, no. 5, pp. 1544–1549.

Chamorro-Premuzic, T., and J. Bersin. July 12, 2018. *4 Ways to Create a Learning Culture on Your Team*. Harvard Business Review Digital Article.

CIPD. 2020. *Creating Learning Cultures: Assessing the Evidence*. London: Chartered Institute of Personnel and Development.

Edmondson, A.C. 2011. "Strategies for Learning From Failure." *Harvard Business Review* 89, no. 4, pp. 48–55.

Garvin, D.A. 1993. "Building a Learning Organization." *Harvard Business Review* 71, no. 4, pp. 78–91.

Garvin, D.A., and L.C. Levesque. 2006. "Meeting Challenges of the Corporate Entrepreneurship." *Harvard Business Review* 84, no. 10, pp. 102–110.

Garvin, D.A., A.C. Edmondson, and F. Gino. 2008. "Is Yours a Learning Organization?" *Harvard Business Review* 86, no. 3, pp. 109–116.

Gharajedaghi, J. 2006. *Systems Thinking: Managing Chaos and Complexity*. Elsevier: San Diego, CA.

Hoogveld, M. 2017. *Agile Management: The Fast and Flexible Approach to Continuous Improvement and Innovation in Organizations*. New York, NY: Business Expert Press.

Joan, B., and V. Joaquim. 2015. "An Innovation Management System to Create Growth in Mature Industrial Technology Firms." *International Journal of Innovation Science* 4. no. 4, pp. 263–280.

Judge, W.Q. 2011. *Organizational Capacity for Change Dimension 5: Systems Thinking*. New York, NY: Business Expert Press.

Kolko, J. 2015. Design Thinking Comes of Age. *Harvard Business Review* 93, no. 9, pp. 66–71.

Kupp, M., J. Anderson, and J. Reckhenrich. 2017. "Why Design Thinking in Business Needs a Rethink." *MIT Sloan Management Review* 59, no. 1, pp. 42–44.

Lemon, K.N., and P.C. Verhoef. 2016. "Understanding Customer Experience Throughout the Customer Journey." *Journal of Marketing* 80, no. 6, pp. 69–96.

López, S.P., J.M.M. Peón, and C.J.V. Ordás. 2006. "Human Resource Management as a Determining Factor in Organizational Learning." *Management Learning* 37, no. 2, pp. 215–239.

Patky, J. 2020. "The Influence of Organizational Learning on Performance and Innovation: A Literature Review." *Journal of Workplace Learning* 32, no. 3, pp. 229–242.

Martel, G., S. Aviron, A. Joannon, E. Lalechère, B. Roche, and H. Boussard. 2017. "Impact of Farming Systems on Agricultural Landscapes and Biodiversity: From Plot to Farm and Landscape Scales." *European Journal of Agronomy* 107, no. 1, pp. 53–62.

Miller, A., and A. Dumford. 2014. "Creative Cognitive Processes in Higher Education." *Journal of Creative Behavior* 50, no. 4, pp. 282–293.

Nakata, C. 2020. "Design Thinking for Innovation: Considering Distinctions, Fit, and Use in Firms. *Business Horizons* 63, no. 6, pp. 763–772.

Norton, B. 2010. "Language and Identity." In N. Hornberger and S. Mckay (eds.), *Sociolinguistics and language education*, pp 349–369. Bristol, Multilingual Matters.

O'Connor, J. 1997. *The Art of Systems Thinking: Essential Skills for Creativity and Problem Solving*. London: Thomson Harper Collins.

Paulus, P.B., and V.R. Brown. 2003. *Enhancing Ideational Creativity in Groups: Lessons From Research on Brainstorming*, pp. 110–136. In P.B. Paulus and B.A. Nijstad (eds.), Group creativity: Innovation through collaboration. Oxford, UK: Oxford University Press.

Prewitt, E. August 01–02, 1998. "Fast Cycle Decision Making." *Harvard Business Publishing Newsletter*.

Quelch, J.A., and E.J. Hoff. 1986. "Customizing Global Marketing." *Harvard Business Review* 64, no. 3, pp. 59–68.

Rajagopal. 2012. *Darwinian Fitness in the Global Marketplace*. Basingstoke: UK: Palgrave Macmillan.

Rajagopal. 2021. "Crowd-Based Business Models—Using Collective Intelligence for Market Competitiveness." Cham, Switzerland: Palgrave Macmillan.

Rajagopal. 2021a. *The Business Design Cube: Converging Markets, Society, and Customer Values to Grow Competitive in Business*. New York, NY: Business Expert Press.

Rajagopal. 2022. *Agile Marketing Strategies: New Approaches to Engaging Consumer Behavior*. New York, NY: Palgrave Macmillan.

Senge, P. 1992. "Building the Learning Organization." *Journal for Quality and Participation* 15, no. 2, pp. 30–38.

Senge, P.M., and G. Carstedt. 2001. "Innovating Our Way to Next Industrial Revolution." *Sloan Management Review* 42, no. 2, pp. 24–38.

Skarzauskiene, A. 2010. "Managing Complexity: Systems Thinking as a Catalyst of the Organization Performance." *Measuring Business Excellence* 14, no. 4, pp. 49–64.

Zheng, W., B. Yang, and G.N. McLean. 2010. "Linking Organizational Culture, Structure, Strategy, and Organizational Effectiveness: Mediating Role of Knowledge Management." *Journal of Business Research* 63, no. 7, pp. 763–771.

CHAPTER 5

Society and Global Business Synergy

This chapter discusses social business modeling and role of transformational leadership in the context of profitability and growth. Social enterprises aim to create both social and financial values, through the people-led business models that allow sustainable growth. These enterprises innovate their business models through multiple activities over time and tailor them to produce social and financial values. In addition, this chapter exhibits synergy pyramid comprising interconnectivity among planning, customer, and strategic alliances. The social consciousness in business has also been discussed in this chapter as an ecosystem of inclusive business, which helps firms tackling poverty and inequality at the BOP segment. The chapter argues that inclusive business generates revenues through social marketing to create social value among stakeholders and surrounding communities. In addition, this chapter discusses the factors affecting the changing consumer behavior and entrepreneurial growth in social business.

Social Business and Entrepreneurship

The social business and entrepreneurship play a significant role in managing social challenges comprising poverty, gender inequality, sustainability and climate change, income disparity, social healthcare, community housing and homelessness, and drive to cleaner food and water supplies across developing economies. There are similarities in entrepreneurial attributes within the socioeconomic, ethnic, and cultural dynamics across these regions. The entrepreneurial ecosystems in the developing economies marginally vary across the PESTEL factors comprising political, economic, social, technological, environmental, and legal perspectives that support the socioeconomic development. The sociocultural dimensions of entrepreneurship in some countries are more catalytic to poverty alleviation and local growth than others (Antonacopoulou and Fuller 2020). Increasing formal businesses in the private and publicly owned firms are largely built on external resources, and it is a difficult proposition to manage enterprises on borrowed resources in developing countries. The underdeveloped markets restrict the growth of these enterprises in developing countries. The growth of informal businesses such as family businesses, and micro-and small enterprises in several developing countries including Argentina, Brazil, Chile, India, Malaysia, Mexico, Nicaragua, Pakistan, South Korea, South Africa, Taiwan, and Turkey have shown slow growth due to resources and market limitations (Guillen 2000). Collective entrepreneurship has emerged as an effective strategy to alleviate extreme poverty. This concept is an outgrowth of inclusive entrepreneurship through which helping the poor integrates as a social process by managing multiple intertwined liabilities of both government and society. Entrepreneurial clusters have been regarded as a possible solution to reduce the incidence of poverty as they can provide the abjectly poor with access to resources, training, and market support. Collective entrepreneurship is a coordinated action to create economic value in the social commons, which holds the unique potential to transfer skills and expertise, hedge against the market risk, and provide support against adverse life circumstances (Kimmitt et al. 2019). However, it has been found that family and community support have a positive effect on micro and small entrepreneurship in rural India and Bangladesh, though the business partners' support is negatively associated with entrepreneurship. Therefore, developing countries have mixed effects on the growth of these enterprises. Thus, entrepreneurship in emerging markets considerably differs from that in developed markets. Digital technologies offer unique entrepreneurial opportunities to overcome the major challenges of poverty in both farm and nonfarm enterprise sectors in emerging markets (Soluk et al. 2021). Entrepreneurship in developing countries has an economic motivation and it is taken up as a survival occupation. Both push and pull factors influence entrepreneurship in low-income demographics. The push-factors include the need for earning, employment, and continuing the family legacy of entrepreneurship, whereas pull-factors include the market attractiveness, market for innovative products, potential market share, need for achievement, autonomy, and financial success. Individuals who are pushed into entrepreneurship are often labeled to be necessity-motivated, and those pulled into entrepreneurship as being opportunity-motivated (Amoros et al. 2021).

Entrepreneurship is a key means through which women can both empower themselves and contribute to prosperous, inclusive, and sustainable development. Although many small and medium-sized enterprises, whether female- and male-owned, face challenges in this respect, women entrepreneurs face constraints toward undermining their potential to contribute to inclusive and sustainable development. Constraints faced by women in the workforce and in the entrepreneurship arena cause high cost for the region's economies. Organized entrepreneurship represents a natural pathway to alleviate poverty. It is arguably a social path to raise per capita income at minimum wages to assure social and personal benefits. Entrepreneurship helps in exploring opportunity for economic advancement and improving the quality of life (Morris et al. 2020). Thailand and the Philippines have notably high level of entrepreneurial activity in all age categories, as well as a significant proportion of the adult population engaged in entrepreneurial activity. Economics of earlier stages of development is often more focused on getting basic requirements in place, while more economically advanced societies attract innovation and entrepreneurship factors like development of a formal venture finance sector and transfer of technology (IDRC 2016). Entrepreneurial activity is influenced by the framework conditions in the environment in which it takes place, and it ultimately benefits this environment through social value and economic development. For example, entrepreneurs create jobs for themselves and others, which creates income for families within the community and improves the quality of life. They develop new products that improve people's lives and advance the knowledge and competitiveness of their societies. Consequently, innovations at various entrepreneurial levels are driven by the sociocultural factors. A regional innovation system helps in developing industrial clusters surrounded by various social organizations. Since innovations occur more frequently in the situation of geographical concentration and proximity, the regional entrepreneurship grows at an economy of scale within the fast-growing knowledge-based economy (Su and Chen 2015).

Previous studies emphasize that women are underrepresented in entrepreneurship in most countries including developed nations, and higher entrepreneurship activity in males explains half the gender gap. The early career entrepreneurship is affected by the existing entrepreneurship among neighbors, family members, and recent schoolmates (Markussen and Roed 2017). Although female entrepreneurship contributes to economic growth, women are less likely to start new ventures compared to men. This gap varies considerably across countries due the entrepreneurial ecosystems and social factors. However, some studies have observed that the rise in female entrepreneurship is due to increased awareness of their role in social and economic development of nations (Brush and Cooper 2012). Despite the importance of female entrepreneurship and growth in the number of female-owned enterprises worldwide, entrepreneurship remains a male-dominated endeavor. Therefore, understanding and exploring the scenario of women entrepreneurship are more important to examine the gender gap in entrepreneurship across nations. The entrepreneurial marketing strategies of entrepreneurs in the emerging markets evolve from social and ethnic entrepreneurial cultures encompassing niche- or regional-marketing strategies. These enterprises largely use bricolage practice in developing marketing strategies. Bricolage is an approach to create new marketing strategies from diverse ecosystems spurring out from the mainstream competitive strategy. The business model for micro and small enterprises is knitted around triadic interrelated dimensions comprising market-driven changes in manufacturing and operational strategies, bootstrapping new portfolios, and effective risk management to drive positive effect on organizational performance (Eggers et al. 2020). The social business and entrepreneurship are affected by various socioeconomic, and push and pull factors that determine the organizational behavior. These factors are illustrated in Figure 5.1.

In inclusive businesses, social entrepreneurship is closely associated with the business goals and performance. Social enterprises, which are founded on the inclusiveness in business, are oriented toward meeting the social challenges such as poverty alleviation and economic empowerment

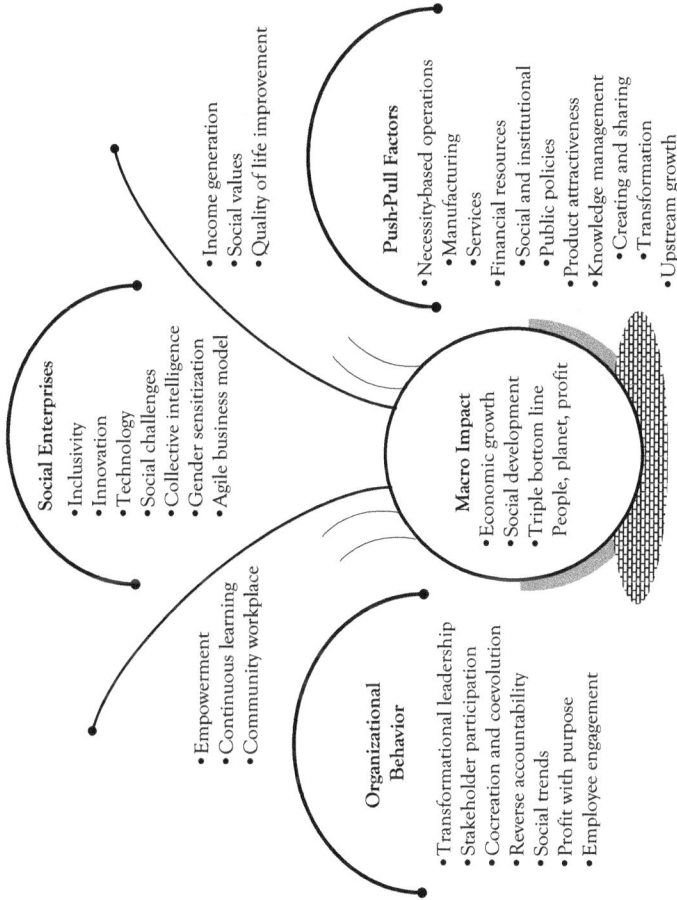

Social Enterprises
- Inclusivity
- Innovation
- Technology
- Social challenges
- Collective intelligence
- Gender sensitization
- Agile business model

- Income generation
- Social values
- Quality of life improvement

Push-Pull Factors
- Necessity-based operations
- Manufacturing
- Services
- Financial resources
- Social and institutional
- Public policies
- Product attractiveness
- Knowledge management
- Creating and sharing
- Transformation
- Upstream growth

- Empowerment
- Continuous learning
- Community workplace

Macro Impact
- Economic growth
- Social development
- Triple bottom line
People, planet, profit

Organizational Behavior
- Transformational leadership
- Stakeholder participation
- Cocreation and coevolution
- Reverse accountability
- Social trends
- Profit with purpose
- Employee engagement

Figure 5.1 Attributes of social business and entrepreneurship

Source: Author

as exhibited in Figure 5.1. Consequently, these enterprises are focused on collective intelligence to manage continuous learning and working with low-cost innovations and technology. Such embedded business objectives drive social enterprises to develop and implement agile business model with autonomy to teams and flexible milestones. The social enterprises have several push and pull factors that influence the organizational behavior. These enterprises undertake necessity bases manufacturing and services operations for upstream growth by managing financial resources through social institutions and aiding through the public programs. The social enterprises largely invest in knowledge management and engage stakeholders in creating and sharing ideas and transforming the conventional business models. The organizational behavior of these enterprises is influenced by the transformational leadership, stakeholder participation, and employee engagement to cocreate innovations and coevolve business. The push and pull factors drive organizations to adapt to the existing social trends and develop *profit with purpose* business goals. One of the salient features of social enterprises is the reverse accountability, which emphasizes organizational governance by the stakeholders.

Latin America is an economically growing region, but entrepreneurship in this region is yet to evolve and develop strong connectivity with the markets. Various social, economic, and internationalization perspectives of entrepreneurship are also under-researched in the region. Many countries in the Latin America have been affected by the economic sluggishness, limitation in technology and innovation, and sociopolitical crises, which significantly affected the entrepreneurial growth (Aguilera et al. 2017). The development of micro-, small-, and medium-sized enterprises are the pillars for economic improvement in many Latin American countries toward generating employment and contributing to economic growth. Even though the contribution of these enterprises would reflect in gross considerable economic growth, these firms are born small and tend to stay small due to lack of dynamic marketing strategies, organizational capabilities, and managerial competencies (Lecuna et al. 2017).

Despite several socioeconomic setbacks, there remain entrepreneurial opportunities. Therefore, it needs a thorough examination of the phenomenon of opportunity seeking, venture development, and growth. The patterns of new venture creation in Latin America have undergone considerable shifts in coping with the technoeconomic changes and adapting to the economic openness to get along the global entrepreneurial and market ecosystem. New venture creation by foreign corporations and by domestic industrial groups in the region has been affected by the low trust perceptions in business and political indifference in Latin America. These factors have affected the financial management processes of existing and new venture creation by jeopardizing the strategic choices and marketing practices (Felzensztein et al. 2015). Digitalization in small and medium enterprises and growth of e-business in Latin America are relatively low as compared to the Asian developing countries, which has delayed the upstream growth and market penetration of these firms. In this context, it would be interesting to explore how corporate alliances and public policies help firms of this region to take advantage of the Industry 4.0 strategies in their efforts to globalize. The implications of the prospects for greater economic and technological integration on decisions for starting businesses will give rise to many marketing and human resource management issues in restructuring and coevolution of small and medium enterprises along with the large firms in Latin American region (Martin and Javalgi 2016).

Entrepreneurship policies, which have supported the start-ups and young firms as potential engines of economic growth and structural transformation, are now widely spread among the general policy agenda in developing countries. Previous studies have observed that innovation in Chile is of desired size, and the market share tends to increase the probability of investment in research and development. However, in most Latin American countries, the incremental innovation and the intensity of research and development by firm size, operations, and investment in innovation activities are limited. Entrepreneurship in Latin America evolves around the niche, while few countries have focused on international markets and adapted to contemporary corporate governance pattern of transitional enterprises (Lopez and Alvarez 2018). Reviewing the social perspective of entrepreneurs in Latin America, it has been observed that women entrepreneurs have shown the potential to engage in social innovation, communication, and transformation of family-oriented businesses. However, women entrepreneurs in technology-based industry face challenges in securing funds and attracting collaborations with multinational companies (Kuschel et al. 2017).

Entrepreneurship at the BOP of the society has emerged as an attribute of subsistence economy in developing countries. The growing number of unstructured micro and small enterprises in the manufacturing and services sectors has increased competition in the niche markets in these countries. However, many new micro enterprises are also emerging in regional marketplaces by creating marginal differentiations in their products and marketing services. The overall entrepreneurial situation in developing and transitional economies has caused chaos leading to cannibalization within the local industries in farm- and nonfarm sectors in general. Such entrepreneurship and market trend have led to new risks in production and business operations related to quality of production, cost-effectiveness, profitability, marketing, and expansion of business by exploring business alliances (Rajagopal 2020). Most micro and small enterprises evolve as family businesses and are owned by individuals. They lack in establishing organizational systems by developing effective backward and forward market networks with business expansion and profitability goals. Such entrepreneurial attributes drive these enterprises more complex to grow. Local enterprises in Asia and Latin America tend to cocreate their products and services with stakeholders to meet the requirements of niche market to generate sustainable customer value. Nonetheless, the individual-driven firms, limited employee engagement, and managerial policies confine these enterprises to a narrow entrepreneurial ecosystem (Herrera-Restrepo and Triantis 2018).

The entrepreneurship in developing countries is also supported by public policies, social institutions, and nongovernmental organizations. The government and social institutions have been encouraging the people-factor in entrepreneurship through the inclusive enterprise concepts in both farm- and nonfarm sectors. The social enterprises in developing countries have been successful in community health, housing, and sustainability activities. However, social accountability toward mixed stakeholders complicates the performance of social enterprises as the measuring standards for social performance are not standardized alike financial performance measurement. Therefore, social enterprises are as complex as the business enterprises in developing countries (Nason et al. 2018). The foundations laid by the sustainability initiatives, investment in social development, and market-based entrepreneurial push have served as powerful enablers of inclusive businesses. Consequently, inclusivity in business has emerged as design-to-society business model to enhance the compatibility between local business and corporate expansion. Besides the social engagement of large companies, inclusive business is also promoted among the small and medium enterprises through business alliances with local firms and cooperatives. Such business models have benefitted the stakeholders and people by integrating them into business value-chains (in the farm and nonfarm sector) in developing economies (e.g., Chamberlain and Anseeuw 2019). Inclusive enterprises are growing selectively across industries and destinations despite most companies addressing the customer needs amid the rising complexities of competition in the market.

Social trends and consumer behavior are continuously changing, and social media is playing a critical role in determining marketing decisions of micro and small enterprises. Volatility of consumption behavior and stakeholder preferences on social enterprises are leaning toward sustainable consumption ecosystem encompassing organic farming and farm products, low-cost housing, effective harnessing of natural resources, and renewable energy to alleviate poverty. Integration of entrepreneurship and inclusivity (role of people) in the implementation of entrepreneurial models helps not only in creating social consciousness to meet the challenges at the grassroots but also in establishing clean production and social governance. The relationship between entrepreneurship and sustainable development is positive. Most micro and small enterprises are transforming by differentiating their products, improving their business designs, and accessing new markets that demand green products (Galindo-Martín et al. 2021). Involving people and engaging customers and stakeholders in the business processes transform companies into learning organizations and make them stay need-based and customer-centric in business. Inclusive businesses operate with diverse workforce and gain abilities in converging divergent business perspectives to develop a social vision for carrying out business with people. People-led firms largely support decision making, idea sharing, and emotions in managing business. Such companies develop abilities to fight conscious and unconscious biases as they coevolve with people and society (Yamk-ovenko and Tavares 2017).

The people-led enterprises have significantly catalyzed the frugal innovation approaches to gain competitive leverage in the *big-middle* consumer segment of developing countries. Such approach has gained momentum in consumer marketing segments. Inclusive businesses could bridge social needs and lead to multiple business outcomes based on *profit with purpose* goals. Many inclusive social businesses led by the technology-based companies (in agriculture, energy, and ecology management sector) have contributed to the long-term sustainabil-ity (Virah-Sawmy 2015). People-led governance in businesses explains how the social vigilance in business organizations helps in controlling unethical moves of the firms for profit at the cost of customers and stake-holders. People's involvement in business also benefits the multistake business model and strengthens multistakeholder mechanism in business governance by co-designing the organizational structures, processes, and principles (Shi 2021). People's participation and social governance have grown over time in promising forms of sharing and leveraging its bene-fits, while circumventing its pitfalls is becoming increasingly important in economic recoveries caused due to the current pandemic.

Social Consciousness

Social conscience, which converges a person's intuitive values with a *mass moral-compass* toward the society in general, can be described as the col-lective value. While rational, sociological, and philosophical arguments often justify that conscience is primarily emotional, but the secondary feelings are associated with community action and values. These emotions help to motivate social choices and behavior, playing an important role in the maintenance and transformation of social norms. These norms are the sum of collective values and priorities of the society. In view of the global pressure on environmental protection and role of companies on manag-ing social responsibility, the corporate sustainability is often considered as a top strategic priority. Companies, however, struggle to link the social responsibility projects with the profitability goals and often fail to gain the stakeholder value. The sustainability-based view of companies suggests that decisions on sustainability projects should be managed through a pyramidal paradigm with interrelated objectives comprising sustainability on the top, and social equity and profitability connected at the BOP in a linear path. Critically, the triple bottom line comprising planet, people, and profit is congruent with the pyramidal paradigm. Accordingly, the corporate sustainability complements the traditional triple bottom approach through social consciousness and motivation to achieve relevant and timely competitive and societal impact (Schneider 2015).

Learning communities are developed by the consumer-centric companies to transfer knowledge on social consumption causes like healthy foods, green consumption, organic farm products, and the like. Such learning communities are designed primarily to increase consumer attitude toward learning new consumption patterns, and building convergence with social, ethnic, and personal values. Companies monitor consumer needs, perceptions, and expectations through the learning communities, and identify marketing strategies, which contributes to augmenting the consumer involvement in learning new consumption experiences and the perceived satisfaction. Digital consumer learning communities do attain positive outcomes; however, consumer education programs need to be developed specific to the requirements of geodemographic segments (Andrade and Cohen 2007). Consumer engagement in companies not only builds high-perceived values among consumers but also helps in developing social consumption behavior. The positive psychodynamics among consumers though social media and interpersonal relations helps in developing pro-brand perceptions, attitude, and behavior. Popular brands try to develop positive perceptions among consumers along the path to purchase, while utility brands influence consumer experience at every touchpoint. Whole Foods in the USA is an example of perceived value-based retailing on organic and sustainable products, which tends to generate consumer consciousness, experience, and organic consumption attitude. Consumers, with the support of growing information technology, view that purchase of organic brands is conventional, while the digital brands are utility brands. The social consciousness is built over time with the growing consumer experience and the accumulated values on organic and sustainable products as socially responsive consumer.

There are several approaches to determine the social environmental consciousness. However, they are united by their common methodological position that embeds the individual and social consciousness toward sustainability in multiple social sectors (agriculture and allied sectors, natural resource management, public health, housing, education, and nonfarm industries). There is a wide range of perspectives concerning social sustainability that need to be supported by the preferences of environmental consciousness. With the increasing social consciousness, global markets have entered the new generation management involving stakeholders in developing customer-centric business strategies and growing sustainable in the competitive marketplace. Consumers form perceptions on the viable solutions to the predetermined needs (recognized as problems), which match with their self-congruence, and could offer sustainable value (satisfaction). Social media is an attractive medium where consumers with changing mindsets interact with peers demonstrating their perceptual rationale and validate their feelings and emotions. Their objective in engaging in social media is to learn about recent trends, new development of knowledge, or certain skill sets for further improvement in making buying decisions (Mathur et al. 2016).

Consumer attitude is a convergence of perceived expectancy and perceived value evolved through the cognitive process of consumer perception. As this convergence becomes stronger over time, it helps in developing consumer attitude toward products and services. Consumer-centric companies observe that sustainable attitudes leverage them toward developing long-term marketing strategies and help them gain enough time and space for implementing these strategies. A sustainable attitude among consumers would lead to cultivating a behavior in due course of time. Consumer perceptions are sensitive to their experiences and help in building attitude if sustained for a reasonable period. Most consumer-centric companies ensure that consumers gain favorable and sustainable perception through brand campaigns, digital communications, and social media forums, and product and services trials. In this perceptual mapping process, the cognitive drivers help consumers in developing sustainable consumer attitude. This situation not only positions the brand as "top-of-mind" element but also encourages repeat buying among the consumers. Although most consumers tend to experiment with low-priced products and substitute the products that deliver satisfactory experience, they fail to develop sustainable perceptions and build attitude toward repeat buying. However, industry attractiveness describes competition among traditional pipeline brands, which succeeds by optimizing the activities in their value chains (Rajagopal 2019).

Danone SA, a French multinational food company based in Paris, has been historically engaged in building social and environmental consciousness as a corporate strategy that focuses on economic and social objectives concerning sustainability. The company categorically considered the social and environmental focus as a part of its decision-making process. Danone communicated its industry-leading efforts to internal and external stakeholders, who were socially conscious about the environment and sustainability. However, over time, the company had learned that it was not enough to have internal systems and data to justify its environmental consciousness. For example, the carbon accounting initiative of the company demonstrated the firm's progress in reducing its carbon footprint. However, the company did not make use of widely accepted carbon accounting standards, which largely discounted its efforts in generating the social values (Arjalies et al. 2018).

Sustainability in social products market is driven by the speed of innovation and technology alongside the trendy products and the changing social values. Companies launch new sustainable products in the competitive marketplace with hedonic or utilitarian values to attract consumers. Consumers develop sustainable perceived use values if the product attractiveness is endorsed by the brand awareness and brand experience. In addition to the newness of products, vogue, social value, ethnic perceptions, and consumer beliefs inculcate the experiential attitude among consumers. Most social-centric companies develop new products as "design-to-value" by involving consumers in cocreation process. Such consumer and stakeholder engagements in new product development help companies manage seasonality of products effectively in the marketplace and develop sustainable consumer attitude and consumption behavior. Therefore, it is observed that like social needs, consumer behavior also turns value-oriented over time. The consumer value chain often supports sustainability and social consciousness.

The first electric hypercar has been manufactured and rolled out in the Indian market, in which it was promoted that the car offers a blend of art and science, in contrast to other hypercars that were designed to appear aggressive and driven completely by the sustainable technology. Anthropomorphism and self-image congruence are associated with the consumers buying behavior. However, building attitude for consumer in marketplace is often more impulsive than judgmental, as attitude is largely determined by the pressure of consumer needs, available choices, and sustainable consumer perceptions. Companies can achieve uniqueness in business strategies by understanding the market trend and the consumer preferences. It is widely believed that continuous management learning helps the managers track market developments and take right decisions to drive the organization in the desired direction. Applied organizational learning is the basic philosophy that underpins the ideas of achieving competencies and capabilities in management of corporate and functional issues (Agnihotri and Bhattacharya 2019). Often, a positive consumption experience guarantees satisfaction, and develops brand loyalty and sustainable behavior among consumers over time. Consumers active on social media also develop knowledge, perceptions, and motivations through the user-generated contents and experience sharing. As social media is dynamic, it attributes to the variable consumer behavior. As innovations in the business-to-consumer and business-to-business segments have shown the tendency of boom and bust, one of the major concerns for the companies carrying out innovative business projects is to make it competitive and sustainable in the marketplace over the spatial and temporal dynamics (Rajagopal 2019). The attributes influencing the social consciousness and organizational behavior are exhibited in Figure 5.2.

Social enterprises are influenced by the extent of social consciousness and stakeholder behavior, which help in building organization behavior in the long run. The attributes of psychosocial factors and social effects on the organizational and business ecosystem are delineated in Figure 5.2. The psychosocial factors are influenced by the collective intelligence and public interactions on the social media channels, which encourage people to develop social self-concept through perceptual semantics and value propositions. Consequently, the social cognition helps in building

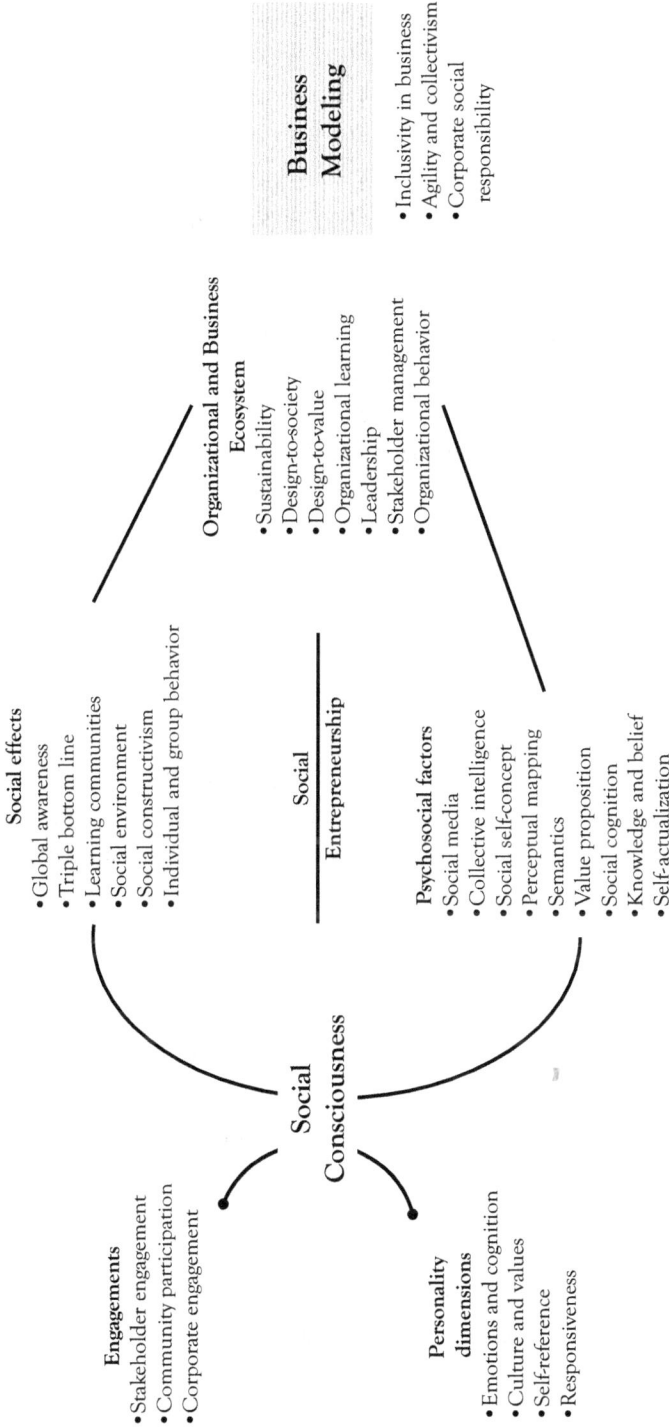

Figure 5.2 Social consciousness and organizational behavior

Source: Author

knowledge and belief among stakeholders in a social enterprise and reveals self-actualization. The psychosocial factors lead to various social effects influenced by the local and global knowledge sharing (awareness), which lead to creation of learning community with the social constructivist philosophy as illustrated in Figure 5.2. The continuous learning and acquisition of knowledge drives individual and group behavior, which induces the business modeling with the organizational and business ecosystem. Consequently, the social and business environment nurtures the triple bottom line by integrating people (stakeholders), planet (sustainability), and profit (business performance). The organizational and business ecosystem focuses on the design-to-society ad design-to-value strategies through transformational leadership and stakeholder management. Accordingly, the social enterprise business modeling encourages inclusivity in business, agility and collectivism in decision-making process, and toward implementing the corporate social responsibility. Broadly, the social consciousness is also driven by the stakeholder and corporate engagements, community participation, and various personality dimensions such as emotions and cognition, culture, values, self-reference, and responsiveness toward society and business.

Consumers are the conscious agents of change in the marketplace, who can alter the demand for existing products and services by identifying and articulating their needs and desires. Consumer-centric companies, thus, invest heavily in mapping consumer cognition and understanding their implicit preferences to revise product designs and make advertising more appealing to them groups (Baumeister et al. 2017). Consumers develop semantic map of values, while analyzing a product through the available verbal and nonverbal information and build knowledge base to support decision process. They systematically estimate the values associated with the products, validate the influencing factors, and compare them with the preferences emerged during the subconscious state of mind by analyzing episodic memories. Consumers drive the realm of choices from the merits of the products and congruence of the episodic memories to construct decision paradigm comprising the products offered, knowledge and influence, subconscious cognition, value determinants, and self-actualization. Such paradigms build cognitive ergonomics and explain a wide array of phenomena in decision making. Distinctive capabilities of the Internet as a platform for customer engagement including interactivity, enhanced reach, persistence, speed, and flexibility suggest that firms can use these capabilities to engage customers in collaborative product innovation through a variety of Internet-based mechanisms. The network mechanisms can facilitate collaborative innovation at different stages of the new product development process and for differing levels of customer involvement (Rajagopal 2019).

Consumers develop perceptions by self-generated stimuli and by drawing inferences from other people in the society. The social perceptions make consumers learn about the feelings and emotions from anchor personalities in the society by analyzing information on physical appearance, and verbal and nonverbal communication. Self-perception by customers relates to values and motivations that drive buying behavior. Visual attraction of products, emotions, self-congruence and perceived experience, knowledge and beliefs, and psychosocial insights about the products drive the perceptions of consumers, which later helps in developing attitude and behavior in future. The consumer philosophy today is woven around the practice of *touch, feel, and pick* of products and services, wherein the perceptual process among consumers is observed in four stages beginning with sensitive feeling, attention, review, and cognitive affirmation. The consumer perception is backed also by ACCA factors comprising awareness, comprehension, conviction, and action. Advertisements, in-store and online promotions, marketing events, referrals, and social media help in generating awareness among consumers to develop self-perceptions on the products and services. Consumers explore further information on the seeded perceptions to comprehend their knowledge and rationale in developing conviction toward the purchase decisions. Conviction is a state of cognition, which builds inclination toward the products or services to buy. Consumer perceptions justified over the conviction may turn into action, as consumers finally buy the products or services (Rajagopal 2011).

Consumers using the social network of relationships to share ideas, experiences, and social perceptions are developed within the niche such as families, common interest groups, interactive societies, and cultures, which profoundly affects social and individual cognition of consumers. The psychodynamic groups with common personality traits and interests function as a microcosm of such social networks. The interactions within these groups support self-actualization process of individuals because of mutual understanding developed during interactions within a cohesive and intimate group. Social constructionists believe that diffusion of information and knowledge transfer can be channelized through the psychodynamic social groups, which help in building the pool of knowledge of everyday life through social interactions. When people interact, they rebuild part of knowledge and induct semantic perceptions as well. Often consumers within the social networks develop experience-based knowledge pools that are close to reality. Such social psychodynamics helps in developing community awareness on new products, reviews, and respected perceptions (Mosek and Gilboa 2016).

Consumer Behavior at the Grassroots

Evaluating human behavioral traits is getting complex today. Society, people, leaders of both social and business forums, and political personalities constitute the external ecosystem of the consumers, which influences their personality and behavioral traits. The social phenotype (William's Syndrome) is related to the personality, social attention, and hypersociability of individuals, which manifests crowd-led influences, dynamic shifts, perceptual inconsistency, and social autism (Thurman and Fisher 2015). The social phenotype behavior of consumers triggers incongruency among corporate assumptions and predictions affecting the consumer personality. Such mismatch leads to failure of the predetermined customer-centric strategies. The social phenotype can be explained as functional behavior of people, which integrates with the neurological functions and alters neurobehavioral traits of people. Consequently, consumers tend to build their consumption behavior on sensitive social moves and neurophysiologically integrated endpoints. Social phenotypes are sensitive to consumption behavior, choices, and loyalty, which can be conceptualized as social intuitive behavior. Firms need to analyze such behavior through psychometric tools to understand consumer perceptions and develop customer centric strategies (Tylka 2006).

One of the principal drivers of consumer behavior is the dominance of social interactions. The involvement of consumers' products depends not only on their own perceptions but also on peers' response to their personality and change proneness. The relation between clothes and identity is perceived by the consumers from the perspective of their values generated in various social interactions. Consumers get involved in exhibiting lifestyle as an aesthetic way of presenting their personality (Pinheiro 2008). In this process, there are both cognitive and affective incentives that translate into potential welfare gains (or indifference) for the consumers in a given social and work-related environment. Customer preference and value placed on designer apparel are largely influenced by social differentiation of the products, and self-esteem of the consumer (Moon et al. 2008). These attributes are likely to vary depending on the customers' cultural orientation. The cultural dimensions of individualism, uncertainty avoidance, power distance, and masculinity should be a useful framework to explain cross-cultural differences in customer acceptance of the designer products. Fashion products are often used for its symbolic value reflecting the personality and status of the user. When the apparel holds a designer brand, it may be perceived as an ostentatious display of wealth. Thus, consumers are motivated by a desire to impress others with their ability to pay particularity high prices for prestigious products (Solomon 1983). Such personality dimensions often play a critical role in shifting the consumer culture toward brand-led buying behavior of utilitarian goods.

Companies need to understand the factors that drive consumer stimuli toward getting associated with new products and brands. The cognitive drivers that affect consumer behavior are listed below:

- Social status to acquire and use specific products
- Self-esteem and personality enhancement
- Making contribution to the society and business by service as lead user and brand ambassador
- Satisfy hedonic value and self-governance
- Stay in public domain and gain social prominence by getting involved in green products and with eco-friendly companies

The role of customer value has been largely recognized over time by the firms as an instrument toward stimulating market share and profit optimization. The customer values for a new product of firm in competitive markets are shaped more by habits, reinforcement effects, and situational influences than strongly held attitudes. The customer value is an intangible factor, which has a significant role in influencing the buying decisions. The lifetime value among customers is built over time by the business firms, which also contributes to the individual perceptions of the customers and augments their value. Purchase intentions in consumers are built by the companies using AATAR tactics and strategies as discussed below:

- Awareness: outreach and frequency of communication, clarity of communication, endorsements on quality and social value of the product by professional associations and celebrities, community education, brand literacy, and peer influence;
- Attributes: Competitive advantages on features of the product, innovation and technology components in the product, sustainable and extended life cycle of products, and high product attractiveness;
- Trial: Product experimentation, adaptability, and perceived use value;
- Availability: Route to market, convenience to customer, and store ambience;
- Repeat buying: brand confidence and loyalty.

The modern market has emerged with the announcement that ethnic dressing comes from the core of the traditional culture, whose gorgeous fabrics have been facelifted as convenience apparel within societal value and lifestyle (VALS) system. It is argued that shifts in consumer culture provide a stimulus to dynamic innovation in the arena of personal taste and consumption. Such dynamism in consumer preferences is considered as a part of an international cultural system and is driven by continuous change in VALS. The consumer values like functionality, fitness for purpose, and efficiency significantly contribute to driving cultural change and recognizing suitable lifestyles (Hartley and Montgomery 2009).

Emotions play an important role in consumer personality and so in their decision making. The influence of consumer emotions and perceptions is complex, as they often turn subtle rather than intense. Emotional reactions are often more persuasive, and short-lived emotions can have lasting effects on their personality and abilities to make decisions. The experience and expression of emotions are often sustainable, reactive, and remembered by the consumers for decision making. Understanding consumer emotions can help managers tailor their strategies to give better prompts to deliver desired response to maximize customer satisfaction and loyalty (Andrade and Capizzani 2011). To portray consumer personality, companies need to observe the cognitive process of consumer choice, beliefs, trust, perceptions, attitude, and behavior carefully, and map their decision touch points. Consumers of a particular company within a brand family experience the similar decision touchpoints and values. Accordingly, companies can understand emotions, rationale, and values of consumers associated with the brands, and develop a cross-functional strategic tool that builds the desired consumer personality (Rosenbaum et al. 2017).

Consumerism is evolved in a society, and businesses are built within the society. Convergence of such relationship between the society and business constructs the consumer behavior. Consequently, collectivism influences consumerism and consumer groups (including individuals), which tend to share consumer experiences on innovations, products, values, and the market developments to generate awareness among the society. The collective opinions influence the purchasers and the society for meeting their needs. Knowledge of consumers' conditions, factors, and behavioral reasons ensures competitiveness in businesses (Sirgy 2018). Companies tend to get closer to the customers by engaging them in cocreating new products and carrying out incremental innovations, improving packaging, developing attractive promotions, and competitive business strategies. Firms aim at attracting emotional customers, so that their bonds with the firms grow deeper. Over time, firms can share emotional experiences with potential customers and motivate their engagement (Das et al. 2019). Consumer behavior is a set of socio-psychological indicators that cultivate a cognitive process in the human beings. It refers to the range of personality attributes exhibited by people, which are influenced by societal values, culture, attitudes, emotions, values, ethics, power, relationships, and persuasion. Behavior in humans is grown as learned, acquired, or shared process over the spatial and temporal factors. Consumer-centric companies periodically map behavioral patterns of consumers by understanding major perceptional and attitudinal patterns, and interpret them to develop appropriate marketing strategies. However, consumer behavior is sensitive to the social dominance, self-esteem, self-actualization, hedonic values, and vogue in the marketplace (Carter and Gilovich 2010).

Various social media channels contribute to disseminating new ideas and serve as a pool of collective intelligence. However, the review of previous literature suggests that the overall effect of crowdsourcing on business modeling has not been thoroughly investigated. This book fills this gap by integrating the customer ideation in developing behavioral business models to achieve *performance with purpose*. Drawing on the resource-based view, the book argues how the crowdsourced information can be an important resource for the firm to develop value-chain, deliver it to stakeholders, and stay competitive in the marketplace (Rajagopal 2021). Socialization of business is a process where people build trust through interpersonal interaction, learn market trends, cocreate products and services, and inculcate the value-based organizational culture. The collective intelligence has evolved over time through the experiential interactions on social media channels. Socialization of businesses encourages people from different segments, sociocultural backgrounds, and ethnicity to cocreate innovative business ideas. The socialization process of business helps firms grow agile and customer-centric (Rajagopal 2021).

With the advancement of technology and convenience-led marketing, elderly consumers are feeling out of place in the market today as they are unable to cope up with the technology-driven marketing approaches, applications, and self-service platforms. Consequently, *reverse socialization* is gearing up in the families as elderly consumers are being influenced by the young consumers. Reverse socialization is a process which allows adolescents influence their parents' knowledge, skills, and attitudes related to consumption. Such behavior is driven by emotions, the changing perceptions on products and services, and restructured cognitive ergonomics (Gentina and Muratore 2012). This book discusses the need for agility in business in the context of reverse sociology, socioneurological behavior, and social self-concept. Individual's cognition on social consumption and relative changes contributes to the social self-concept, which determines the buying decisions and the relative degree of influence (Singh et al. 2020). Research studies converging behavioral and neural mechanisms in social media use and self-concept indicate that the cognitive weights between self-judgments and derived peer judgments are often narrow and highly correlated. Social media enables consumers to get more frequent crowd-based feedback as compared to interpersonal interactions and conventional meetings with peers. Consequently, the social media drives peer emotions in socialization of business among young consumers (Valkenburg 2017).

The crowd's value to the firm is represented as the concept of *crowd capital*, which embeds customer perceptions and emotions. The crowd capital has been defined as organizational resources acquired through crowdsourcing in the form of collective intelligence (Prpić et al. 2015). Most companies have experimented radical shifts in business strategies over the conventional wisdom to gain sustainable competitive advantage. Some of these strategies are people-centric and crowd-based, which have encouraged customer engagement in today's heterogeneous and hyper-competitive global business environment. Consequently, empowering people in various geodemographic segments (communities, entrepreneurs, women, and leaders) has gained dynamic capabilities such as sensing local opportunities, enacting global complementarities, and appropriating business with local values. Nestlé (Latin America), Unilever (India), and IKEA (Europe) are some good examples of the companies engaged in people-based business. These companies can operate successfully across emerging and established markets. The strategic agility, therefore, is a meta-capability of companies that enables them to create customer and stakeholder values and deploy dynamic competitive strategies in a balance over time (Fourne et al. 2014).

Companies of 20th century have long used teams to solve problems, take decisions, and develop business models. Market research organizations have heavily focused on investigating groups to explore customer needs, and conducted consumer surveys to understand the market, while managers have kept themselves busy in attending business meetings to listen to shareholders in the past. But the words that need more comprehension such as *solve, explore, understand,* and *listen* have now taken on a whole new meaning through the technology platforms to acquire and analyze collective (crowdsourced) opinions on a larger scale. Indeed, the increasing use of market information, free encyclopedias, crowdsourcing tools, the *wisdom of crowd* concepts, social networks, collaborative software, and other Web-based tools push a paradigm shift for companies in making customer-centric decisions (Bonabeau 2008). Crowdsourcing has emerged as a creative tool for companies today to expand their outreach to customers, map their perceptions, and understand behavioral implications of customers in business. Thus, this tool has led to deliver collective intelligence, which helps the companies in building the business design cube by integrating the concepts of design-to-market, design-to-society, and design-to-value in business modeling process. Cocreation allows companies to continually tap the skills and insights of stakeholders and develop new ways of building value-chain. Crowdsourcing platforms (physical and digital forums) are largely interactive for exploring new experiences and connections. The crowd-based collective intelligence process grows organically over time in the organization as a system (Gouillart and Billings 2013).

Consumer emotions are largely set through the verbal and nonverbal market communications extended by the companies. Advertisements play a critical role in stimulating the consumer emotions. Right from the late 20th century, as the usage of computers has rapidly grown, the Internet has been the prime anchor of the marketing communications and stimulant of consumer emotions. The increased participation of people on the social network platforms has brought the emotions associated with the products, services, and companies very close to the market players. Compared to the offline media communications, social network platforms possess unique characteristics that affect the likelihood of generating emotions and reactions to the experience on the brand among the fellow customers and employees of the firm. The online emotion is largely driven by the vividness of social networks, interactivity, challenge, interaction speed, machine memory, and allowable social interactions. Depending on how a social network platform performs on these dimensions, positive or negative emotions may result on the products, services, or on the image of the company. For example, using machine memory to automatically generate purchase recommendations based on the prior consumption patterns

may be perceived as pleasantly surprising, while a firm sending unsolic-
ited e-mails based on a user's cookie trail may be annoying. Such feelings
generated and shared by the consumers get attached to the brand and
build its equity in the market. Thus, the challenge of the brand managers is to get consumers to associate positive emotions with a brand and
manage company-sponsor's social network websites by understanding the
consumer emotions and their ramifications (Jones et al. 2008).

Consumer arousal is largely driven by the acquired emotions through
crowd behavior, collective intelligence, or corporate influence. The collective intelligence also stimulates the neurobehavior of consumers in a
specific situation. The consumer emotions subsequently affect pleasure
and shopping behaviors such as buying intention and buying eagerness
among consumers. Consumers get motivated by the in-store demonstra-
tions, fellow customers, social media influencers, and self-reference criteria for shopping specific products and drive motivational arousal and
merriment on products. The social values and lifestyle also motivate the
hedonic desire among consumers, and they look for acquiring products of
self-congruence. Consequently, the derived arousal has a positive effect on
pleasure and associated emotions. Contrary to hedonic emotions when
consumers have a utilitarian motivational orientation, arousal has a mild
effect on pleasure. Consumers have a utilitarian motivational orientation
when their behaviors are directed toward products, services, and activities
that they perceive as "must do," and are not intrinsically rewarding. Consequently, consumers with a utilitarian motivational orientation try to
complete their task as efficiently as possible with the minimum cost and
mental stress (Vieira and Torres 2014).

Social Business Modeling

Social values are built on cultural dimensions and ethnicity. Egalitarianism
and embeddedness of consumers in the society affect the business environment. Companies, thus, develop social welfare policies as corporate
social responsibilities, and build consumer values. Moreover, social values
affect the individual ideological orientation on consumer attitudes toward
industry, government policies, and consumer behavior (Arikan and
Bloom 2014). Technology shows significant positive impact on economic

growth, while both human capital and technology are the important determinants of growth in developing countries and emerging markets. Therefore, improvement of the educational sector and more funding for research and development among developing countries are some prominent considerations for monitoring and measuring business growth. Such conditions encourage innovations needed to facilitate sustained economic growth (Adelakun 2011).

Most companies implement CSR projects in association with the informal social groups, knows as self-help groups (SHGs). Women's SHGs in India provide an interesting and concrete example of an intervention that is well aligned with theoretical ideas about development as a process of capability expansion. These groups contribute to the policy priorities of gender empowerment laid in the global sustainability development goals. The JEEVikA (livelihood) program in Bihar, India, finds that economically and socially marginalized groups have been benefited from SHG membership through a reduction in reliance on high-cost sources of borrowing. These SHGs have helped to increase the participation of women in household decision making and delivered positive impacts on human development in rural areas. Similarly, another SHG in Andhra Pradesh, a southern state in India, has evidenced impact on enhancing social capital as the organization has motivated program members on higher savings to move freely within their village and interact within their caste. Protein and energy intake, and consumption also increased among member of the group as their income or assets changed. These groups establish sustainability in human development and rural wealth generation (Anand et al. 2019).

Social capital, which is an asset in improving the knowledge of stakeholders, positively affects purchase intention of consumers toward organic foods and stimulates actual purchase behavior. Contemporary knowledge and experience sharing among women in interpersonal or digital platforms help in developing trust on the acquired knowledge. The social capital includes the following dimensions that help in promoting community participation and stakeholder engagement:

- Interpersonal relationships
- Functional support through social networks

- Stakeholder engagement
- Trust and cooperation

Trust significantly mediates the relationship between available information, perceived knowledge, and organic purchase intentions. Attitudes toward organic foods and subjective norms also significantly influence organic food choices among women consumers (Teng and Wang 2015). Social influence and perceived knowledge develop cognition in the form of beliefs, utilitarian attitudes, and behavior toward consumption of organic products. Women also feel hedonic pleasure in paying premium price for organic products to cater to health and family wellness needs (Lee and Goudeau 2014). The successful adaptation and creation of sustainable entrepreneurial ventures are significantly influenced by the interactions within social networks (tradition and digital), which augment the ability to create collective intelligence, and environmentally and socially integrated economic systems. Sustainable business models are largely driven by the social networks and stakeholders at the mature stage of businesses, as they rely more on social patronage and values than corporate sponsorship. However, the development of sustainable business models is a complex process that requires a supportive entrepreneurial and social ecosystem (Neumeyer and Santos 2018).

Social impact theory (SIT) also explains the contextual association of an individual's decision making within the social values and influences behavioral perspectives. Major behavioral theories, therefore, focus on proximal influences on behavior that are instrumental in developing cognitive attributes within the social context. Attributes of SIT delineate how emotions shift the focus of an individual's decision making to the wider context of social relations and guide the subjectivity norms such as hedonism, anthropomorphism, and self-esteem among individuals. Social interactions embedded in social commerce sites and media channels influence the purchase intention. Positive interpersonal communication and user-generated contents on digital platforms significantly affect consumers' intention to buy a product. Intention to purchase driven by social interaction facilitates the likelihood of actual buying and sharing information with peers (Wang and Yu 2017). Many companies diagnose social problems with an engineering mindset to build it the right way and make sure it works. During this process, the social and cultural intentions are often ignored, which result into delays in adaptation to the solutions. Eco-innovations, on the other hand, approach problems with the question as we are integrating the social values in the prototype and building the right solution in the first place? Combining imagination, insights, and impact in providing a right ecological solution emerges as a major challenge to the companies.

The community creation model in managing renewable businesses projects across the downstream market comprising rural household and farm and nonfarm sectors functions more as social governance than a corporate venture. The governance mechanism for managing green energy projects in the rural areas lies between the hierarchy-based (closed) mechanism and the market-based (open) systems. However, success of green energy projects in developing economies spreads faster across the social block-chains driving butterfly effect. Community-centric model shifts the focus of innovation and drives the change process beyond the boundaries of the firm, to a community of individuals and firms that collaborate to create joint intellectual property. Such strategies involve community in diffusing the change instituted by the company and set ground rules for participation and developing sustainable consumer behavior with differentiation. Community creation model allows innovation-led changes to initially pass through a complex environment by striking a balance between order and chaos in the market (Sawhney and Prandelli 2000).

Administrative complexities play a significant role in explaining new technology drive. Process simplification, zero defect products, cost and profit, and overall governance of new products development have many odds to be either eliminated or managed within the organizational system. Most SHGs do not set up innovation platforms foreseeing the odds and complexities, nor think about them during the process, and give up the business process. Such behavior is significantly affected by the perception of administrative complexity. The technology marketing grid has several factors that pose conflicts and challenges to the innovation and technology development firms during different levels of the process. The complexity grid comprises 12 commonly observed points of conflicts, with independent effects of each point as well as in a matrix form (Rajagopal 2016). The conflict points in the grid include following factors:

- Ideation
- Resources management
- Process management
- Capabilities and competencies
- Technology marketing
- Growth and next generation innovation and technology issues
- Involvement
- Organizational policies
- Operational efficiency
- Competitive decision
- Business environment
- Organizational culture

The aforementioned factors nurture the innovation and technology development projects in the firm. In the complexity grid ideation process, the extent of involvement of employees, consumers, and market players creates cognitive and organizational conflicts and challenges. On the other hand, management of resources and organizational policies raises various challenging issues during the different phases of innovation and technology development.

References

Adelakun, O.J. 2011. "Human Capital Development and Economic Growth in Nigeria." *European Journal of Business and Management* 3, no. 9, pp. 29–39.

Agnihotri, A., and S. Bhattacharya. 2019. *Vazirani Shul: India's First Electric Hypercar*. London, ON, Canada: Ivey Business School Press.

Aguilera,R.V., L. Ciravegna, A. Cuervo-Cazurra, and M.A. Gonzalez-Perez. 2017. "Multilatinas and the Internationalization of Latin American Firms." *Journal of World Business* 52, no. 4, pp. 447–460.

Amorós, J.E., O. Cristi, and W. Naudé. 2021. "Entrepreneurship and Subjective Well-Being: Does the Motivation to Start-Up a Firm Matter?" *Journal of Business Research* 217,pp. 389–398.

Anand, P., S. Saxena, R. Gonzalez, and H.H. Dang. 2019. *Can Women's Self-Help Groups Contribute to Sustainable Development? Evidence of Capability Changes From Northern India*. Policy Research Working Paper #9011, Washington, DC: World Bank Group.

Andrade, E.B., and J.B. Cohen. 2007. "On the Consumption of Negative Feeling." *Journal of Consumer Research* 34, no. 3, pp. 283–300.

Andrade, E.B., and M. Capizzani. 2011. *Emotional Cues That Work Magic on Customers*. Cambridge, MA: Harvard Business School Publication.

Antonacopoulou, E., and T. Fuller. 2020. "Practicing Entrepreneuring as Emplacement: The Impact of Sensation and Anticipation in Entrepreneurial Action." *Entrepreneurship & Regional Development* 32, no. 3–4, pp. 257–280.

Arjalies, D.L., M. Rodrigue, D. Gibassier, and K. Mark. 2018. *Danone: Adopting Integrated Reporting or Not? (A)*. Boston, MA: Harvard Business School Press.

Arikan, G., and P.B. Bloom. 2014. "Social Values and Cross-National Differences in Attitudes Towards Welfare." *Political Studies* 63, no. 2, pp. 431–448.

Baumeister, R.F., C.J. Clark, J. Kim, and S. Lau. 2017. "Consumers (and Consumer Researchers) Need Conscious Thinking in Addition to Unconscious Processes: A Call for Integrative Models, a Commentary on Williams and Poehlman." *Journal of Consumer Research* 44, no. 2, pp. 252–257.

Bonabeau, E. 2008. "Decisions 2.0: The Power of Collective Intelligence." *MIT Sloan Management Review* 50, no. 2, pp. 45–52.

Brush, C.G., and S.Y. Cooper. 2012. "Female Entrepreneurship and Economic Development: An International Perspective." *Entrepreneurship & Regional Development* 24, no. 1–2, pp. 1–6.

Carter, T.J., and T. Gilovich. 2010. "The Relative Relativity of Experiential and Material Purchases." *Journal of Personality and Social Psychology* 98, no. 1, pp. 146–159.

Chamberlain, W., and W. Anseeuw. 2019. "Inclusiveness Revisited: Assessing Inclusive Businesses in South African Agriculture." *Development Southern Africa* 36, no. 5, pp. 600–615.

Das, G., J. Agarwal, N.K. Malhotra, and G. Varshneya. 2019. "Does Brand Experience Translate Into Brand Commitment? A Mediated-Moderation Model of Brand Passion and Perceived Brand Ethicality." *Journal of Business Research* 95, pp. 479–490.

Eggers, F., T. Neimand, S. Kraus, and M. Breier. 2020. "Developing a Scale for Entrepreneurial Marketing: Revealing Its Inner Frame and Prediction of Performance," *Journal of Business Research* 113, pp. 72–82.

Felzensztein, C., L. Ciravegna, P. Robson, and J.E. Amorós. 2015. "Networks, Entrepreneurial Orientation, and Internationalization Scope: Evidence From Chilean Small and Medium Enterprises." *Journal of Small Business Management* 53, no. S1, pp. 145–160.

Fourne, S.P.L., J.J.P. Jansen, and T.J.M. Mom. 2014. "Strategic Agility in MNEs: Managing Tensions to Capture Opportunities Across Emerging and Established Markets." *California Management Review* 56, no. 3, pp. 13–38.

Galindo-Martín, M.A., M.S. Castaño-Martínez, and M.T. Méndez-Picazo. 2021. "Effects of the Pandemic Crisis on Entrepreneurship and Sustainable Development." *Journal of Business Research* 137, pp. 345–353.

Gentina, E., and I. Muratore. 2012. "Environmentalism at Home: The Process of Ecological Resocialization by Teenagers." *Journal of Consumer Behaviour* 11, no. 2, pp. 162–169.

Gouillart, F., and D. Billings. 2013. "Community-Powered Problem Solving." *Harvard Business Review* 91, no. 4, pp. 70–77.

Guillen, M.F. 2000. "Business Groups in Emerging Economies: A Resource-Based View." *Academy of Management Journal* 43, no. 3, pp. 362–380.

Hartley, J., and L. Montgomery. 2009. "Fashion as Consumer Entrepreneurship: Emergent Risk Culture, Social Network Markets, and the Launch of *Vogue* in China." *Chinese Journal of Communication* 2, no. 1, pp. 61–76.

Herrera-Restrepo, O., and K. Triantis. 2018. "Enterprise Design Through Complex Adaptive Systems and Efficiency Measurement." *European Journal of Operational Research* 278, no. 2, pp. 481–497.

IDRC. 2016. *Asian Regional Entrepreneurship Report (2015–16)*. Kulalumpur.

Jones, M.Y., M.T. Spence, and C. Vallester. 2008. "Creating Emotions Via B to C Websites." *Business Horizons* 51, no. 5, pp. 419–428.

Kimmitt, J., P. Muñoz, and R. Newbery. 2019. "Poverty and the Varieties of Entrepreneurship in the Pursuit of Prosperity." *Journal of Business Venture* 35, no. 4, pp. 1–18.

Kuschel, K., M.T. Lepeley, F. Espinosa, and S. Gutierrez. 2017. "Funding Challenges of Latin American Women Start-Up Founders in the Technology Industry." *Cross Cultural and Strategic Management* 24, no. 2, pp. 310–331.

Lecuna, A., B. Cohen, and R. Chavez. 2017. "Characteristics of High-Growth Entrepreneurs in Latin America." *International Entrepreneurship and Management Journal* 13, no. 1, pp. 141–159.

Lee, H.J., and C. Goudeau. 2014. "Consumers' Beliefs, Attitudes, and Loyalty in Purchasing Organic Foods: The Standard Learning Hierarchy Approach." *British Food Journal* 116, no. 6, pp. 918–930.

Lopez, T., and C. Alvarez. 2018. "Entrepreneurship Research in Latin America: A Literature Review." *Academia Revista Latinoamericana de Administracion* 31, no. 4, pp. 736–756.

Markussen, S., and K. Roed. 2017. "The Gender Gap in Entrepreneurship—The Role of Peer Effects." *Journal of Economic Behavior & Organization* 134, pp. 356–373.

Morris, M.H., S.C. Santos, and X. Neumeyer. 2020. "Entrepreneurship as a Solution to Poverty in Developed Economies." *Business Horizons* 63, no. 3, pp. 377–390.

Martin, S.L., and. R.R.G. Javalgi. 2016. "Entrepreneurial Orientation, Marketing Capabilities and Performance: The Moderating Role of Competitive Intensity on Latin American International New Ventures." *Journal of Business Research* 69, no. 6, pp. 2040–2051.

Moon, J., D. Chadee, and S. Tikoo. 2008. "Culture, Product Type, and Price Influences on Consumer Purchase Intention to Buy Personalized Products Online." *Journal of Business Research* 61, no. 1, pp. 31–39.

Mosek, A.A., and R.B. Gilboa. 2016. "Integrating Art in Psychodynamic-Narrative Group Work to Promote the Resilience of Caring Professionals." *The Arts in Psychotherapy* 51, pp. 1–9.

Nason, R.S., S. Bacq, and D. Gras. 2018. "A Behavioral Theory of Social Performance: Social Identity and Stakeholder Expectations." *Academy of Management Review* 43, pp. 259–283.

Neumeyer, X., and S.C. Santos. 2018. "Sustainable Business Models, Venture Typologies, and Entrepreneurial Ecosystems: A Social Network Perspective." *Journal of Cleaner Production* 172, pp. 4565–4579.

Pinheiro, M. 2008. "Loyalty, Peer Group Effects, and 401(k)." *The Quarterly Review of Economics and Finance* 48, no. 1, pp. 94–122.

Prpić, J., P.P. Shukla, J.H. Kietzmann, and I.P. McCarthy. 2015. "How to Work a Crowd: Developing Crowd Capital Through Crowdsourcing." *Business Horizons* 58, no. 1, pp. 77–85.

Rajagopal. 2011. "Determinants of Shopping Behavior of Urban Consumers." *International Journal of Consumer Marketing* 23, no. 2, pp. 83–104.

Rajagopal. 2016. *Innovative Business Projects: Breaking Complexities, Building Performance (Vol. 1)-Fundamentals and Project Environment.* New York, NY: Business Expert Press.

Rajagopal. 2019. *Contemporary Marketing Strategy: Analyzing Consumer Behavior to Drive Managerial Decision Making.* New York, NY: Palgrave Macmillan.

Rajagopal, A. 2020. *Managing Startup Enterprises in Emerging Markets: Leadership Dynamics and Marketing Strategies.* New York, NY: Palgrave Macmillan.

Rajagopal. 2021. *Crowd-Based Business Models-Using Collective Intelligence for Market Competitiveness.* New York, NY: Palgrave Macmillan.

Rosenbaum, M., M.L. Otalora, and G.C. Ramirez. 2017. "How to Create a Realistic Customer Journey Map." *Business Horizons* 60, no. 1, pp. 143–150.

Sawhney, M., and E. Prandelli. 2000. "Communities of Creation: Managing Distributed Innovation in Turbulent Markets." *California Management Review* 42, no. 4, pp. 24–54.

Schneider, A. 2015. "Reflexivity in Sustainability Accounting and Management: Transcending the Economic Focus of Corporate Sustainability." *Journal of Business Ethics* 127, no. 3, pp. 525–536.

Shi, H. 2021. "The Application of Social Psychology and Collective Internet Governance." *Aggression and Violent Behavior*. (*in Press*). https://doi.org/10.1016/j.avb.2021.101588

Singh, P., S. Sahadev, C.J. Oates, and P. Alevizou. 2020. "Pro-Environmental Behavior in Families: A Reverse Socialization Perspective." *Journal of Business Research* 115, pp. 110–121.

Sirgy, M.J. 2018. "Self-Congruity Theory in Consumer Behavior: A Little History." *Journal of Global Scholars of Marketing Science* 28, no. 2, pp. 197–207.

Solomon, M.R. 1983. "The Role of Products as Social Stimuli: A Symbolic Interactionist Perspective." *Journal of Consumer Research* 10, pp. 319–329.

Soluk, J., N. Kammerlander, and S. Darwin. 2021. "Digital Entrepreneurship in Developing Countries: The Role of Institutional Voids." *Technological Forecasting and Social Change* 170. https://doi.org/10.1016/j.techfore.2021.120876

Su, Y.S., and J. Chen. 2015. "Introduction to Regional Innovation Systems in East Asia." *Technological Forecasting and Social Change* 100, pp. 80–82.

Teng, C.C., and Y.M. Wang. 2015. "Decisional Factors Driving Organic Food Consumption: Generation of Consumer Purchase Intentions." *British Food Journal* 117, no. 3, pp. 1066–1081.

Thurman, A.J., and M.H. Fisher. 2015. "The Williams Syndrome Social Phenotype: Disentangling the Contributions of Social Interest and Social Difficulties." In R.M. Hodapp and D.J. Fidler. (eds), *International Review of Research in Developmental Disabilities*, pp. 191–227. Amsterdam: Academic Press.

Tylka, T.L. 2006. "Development and Psychometric Evaluation of a Measure of Intuitive Eating." *Journal of Consumer Psychology* 53, pp. 226–240.

Virah-Sawmy, M. 2015. "Growing Inclusive Business Models in the Extractive Industries: Demonstrating a Smart Concept to Scale Up Positive Social Impacts." *The Extractive Industries and Society* 2, no. 4, pp. 676–679.

Vieira, V.A., and C.V. Torres. 2014. "The Effect of Motivational Orientation Over Arousal-Shopping Response Relationship." *Journal of Retailing and Consumer Services* 21, no. 2, pp. 158–167.

Valkenburg, P.M. 2017. "Understanding Self-Effects in Social Media." *Human Communication Research* 43, pp. 477–490.

Wang, Y., and C. Yu. 2017. "Social Interaction-Based Consumer Decision-Making Model in Social Commerce: The Role of Word of Mouth and Observational Learning." *International Journal of Information Management* 37, no. 3, pp. 179–189.

Yamkovenko, B., and S. Tavares. 2017. *To Understand Whether Your Company Is Inclusive, Map How Your Employees Interact*. Harvard Business Review Digital Article, Cambridge, MA: Harvard Business School Press.

About the Author

Rajagopal is Professor of Marketing at EGADE Business School of Monterrey Institute of Technology and Higher Education (ITESM), Mexico City Campus and Life Fellow of the Royal Society for Encouragement of Arts, Manufacture and Commerce, London. Dr. Rajagopal is Visiting Professor at Boston University, Boston, Massachusetts. He has been listed with biography in various international directories. He is serving also as Visiting Professor at University of Fraser Valley, British Columbia, Canada-India Campus.

He offers courses in the areas of marketing, innovation management, and international business to the students of undergraduate, graduate, and doctoral programs. He has imparted training to senior executives and has conducted over 70 management development programs to the corporate executives and international faculty. Throughout his career, Dr. Rajagopal has delivered a number of courses and executive and doctoral programs regarding the areas of marketing and international business in Business Schools including Indian Institute of Management, at Indore and Rohtak, India; Narsee Monjee Institute of Management Studies, Mumbai, Institute of Public Enterprise, Hyderabad, India, and at International Management Institute, Bhubaneswar, India.

Rajagopal holds postgraduate and doctoral degrees in Economics and Marketing, respectively, from Ravishankar University in India. He has to his credit 68 books on marketing and innovation management themes and over 400 research contributions that include published research papers in national and international refereed journals. He is Editor-in-Chief of International Journal of Leisure and Tourism Marketing and International Journal of Business Competition and Growth. Dr. Rajagopal served as Associate Editor of Emerald Emerging Markets Case Studies during the period 2012 to 2019. Rajagopal is also serving as Book Series Editor for the Palgrave Studies of Entrepreneurship and Social Challenges in Developing Economies. He is on the editorial board of various journals of international repute.

The research contributions of Rajagopal have been recognized by the National Council of Science and Technology (CONACyT), Government of Mexico by awarding him the honor of the highest level of National Researcher-SNI Level-III. He has been awarded UK-Mexico Visiting Chair 2016–2017 for collaborative research on "Global-Local Innovation Convergence" with University of Sheffield, UK, instituted by the Consortium of Higher Education Institutes of Mexico and UK.

Index

OTHER TITLES IN THE SERVICE SYSTEMS AND INNOVATIONS IN BUSINESS AND SOCIETY COLLECTION

Jim Spohrer, IBM, and Haluk Demirkan, University of Washington, Tacoma, Editors

- *Service in the AI Era* by Jim Spohrer, Paul P. Maglio, Stephen L. Vargo, and Markus Warg
- *The Emergent Approach to Strategy* by Peter Compo
- *Compassion-Driven Innovation* by Nicole Reineke, Debra Slapak, and Hanna Yehuda
- *Adoption and Adaption in Digital Business* by Keith Sherringham and Bhuvan Unhelkar
- *Customer Value Starvation Can Kill* by Walter Vieira
- *Build Better Brains* by Martina Muttke
- *ATOM, Second Edition* by Kartik Gada
- *Designing Service Processes to Unlock Value, Third Edition* by Joy M. Field
- *Disruptive Innovation and Digital Transformation* by Marguerite L. Johnson
- *Service Excellence in Organizations, Volume II* by Fiona Urquhart
- *Service Excellence in Organizations, Volume I* by Fiona Urquhart
- *Obtaining Value from Big Data for Service Systems, Volume II* by Stephen H. Kaisler, Armour, and J. Alberto Espinosa
- *Obtaining Value from Big Data for Service Systems, Volume I* by Stephen H. Kaisler, Armour, and J. Alberto Espinosa

Concise and Applied Business Books

The Collection listed above is one of 30 business subject collections that Business Expert Press has grown to make BEP a premiere publisher of print and digital books. Our concise and applied books are for...

- Professionals and Practitioners
- Faculty who adopt our books for courses
- Librarians who know that BEP's Digital Libraries are a unique way to offer students ebooks to download, not restricted with any digital rights management
- Executive Training Course Leaders
- Business Seminar Organizers

Business Expert Press books are for anyone who needs to dig deeper on business ideas, goals, and solutions to everyday problems. Whether one print book, one ebook, or buying a digital library of 110 ebooks, we remain the affordable and smart way to be business smart. For more information, please visit www.businessexpertpress.com, or contact sales@businessexpertpress.com.

www.ingramcontent.com/pod-product-compliance
Lightning Source LLC
Chambersburg PA
CBHW061304220326
41599CB00026B/4723